Preface

Microsoft Azure Network Engineer AZ 700: Designing and Implementing Microsoft Azure Networking Solutions is a meticulously structured guide designed to equip network engineers and IT professionals with the essential knowledge and technical proficiency required to design, implement, and manage Azure-based networking solutions. As cloud adoption accelerates across industries, the ability to build and maintain secure, scalable, and highly available network architectures has become a critical skill. This book is aligned with the objectives of the AZ-700 certification exam, covering fundamental and advanced networking concepts such as Azure Virtual Networks, VPN Gateways, hybrid networking, load balancing, network security, and monitoring solutions. Through a structured learning approach, each chapter progressively builds upon core concepts, ensuring a comprehensive understanding of Azure networking principles and best practices for real-world implementation.

Beyond serving as a certification study guide, Microsoft Azure Network Engineer AZ 700: Designing and Implementing Microsoft Azure Networking Solutions is a valuable resource for professionals seeking to enhance their expertise in cloud networking. Each chapter integrates practical exercises, real-world case studies, and review questions to reinforce learning and facilitate knowledge retention. Additionally, supplementary resources such as online test papers and expert-led video tutorials further enrich the learning experience, bridging the gap between theoretical knowledge and practical application. Whether you are preparing for the AZ-700 exam or looking to expand your capabilities in designing and managing Azure networking solutions, this book provides the structured guidance necessary to excel in one of the most vital domains of cloud computing.

Table of Contents

Chapter 1: Practice Questions & Answers Part 1

QUESTION 1
You need to provide connectivity to storage1. The solution must meet the PaaS networking requirements and the business requirements.
What should you include in the solution?
A. a service endpoint
B. Azure Front Door
C. a private endpoint
D. Azure Traffic Manager
Answer: A

QUESTION 2
You create NSG10 and NSG11 to meet the network security requirements.
For each of the following statements, select Yes it the statement is true. Otherwise, select No.
NOTE: Each correct selection is worth one point.
A. Mastered
B. Not Mastered
Answer: A

QUESTION 3
- (Exam Topic 2)
What should you implement to meet the virtual network requirements for the virtual machines that connect to Vnet4 and Vnet5?
A. a private endpoint
B. a virtual network peering
C. a private link service
D. a routing table
E. a service endpoint
Answer: B
A. Mastered
B. Not Mastered
Answer: A

QUESTION 4
- (Exam Topic 3)
You have 10 Azure App Service instances. Each instance hosts the same web app. Each instance is in a different Azure region.
You need to configure Azure Traffic Manager to direct users to the instance that has the lowest latency. Which routing method should you use?
A. geographic
B. weighted
C. performance
D. priority
Answer: D

QUESTION 5
- (Exam Topic 3)
You have an Azure Front Door instance named FD1 that is protected by using Azure Web Application Firewall (WAF).
FD1 uses a frontend host named app1.contoso.com to provide access to Azure web apps hosted in the East US Azure region and the West US Azure region.
You need to configure FD1 to block requests to app1.contoso.com from all countries other than the United States.
What should you include in the WAF policy?
A. a frontend host association
B. a managed rule set
C. a custom rule that uses a rate limit rule
D. a custom rule that uses a match rule
Answer: C

QUESTION 6
- (Exam Topic 3)
You are planning the IP addressing for the subnets in Azure virtual networks. Which type of resource requires IP addresses in the subnets?
A. Azure Virtual Network NAT
B. virtual network peering
C. service endpoints
D. private endpoints
Answer: A

QUESTION 7
- (Exam Topic 3)
You have an Azure virtual network named Vnet1 that has one subnet. Vnet1 is in the West Europe Azure region.
You deploy an Azure App Service app named App1 to the West Europe region.
You need to provide App1 with access to the resources in Vnet1. The solution must minimize costs. What should you do first?
A. Create a private link.
B. Create a new subnet.
C. Create a NAT gateway.
D. Create a gateway subnet and deploy a virtual network gateway.
Answer: B

QUESTION 8
- (Exam Topic 3)
You have an Azure Traffic Manager parent profile named TM1. TM1 has two child profiles named TM2 and TM3.
TM1 uses the performance traffic-routing method and has the endpoints shown in the following table.
TM2 uses the weighted traffic-routing method with MinChildEndpoint = 2 and has the endpoints shown in the following table.

TM3 uses priority traffic-routing method and has the endpoints shown in the following table.
The App2, App4, and App6 endpoints have a degraded monitoring status.
To which endpoint is traffic directed? To answer, select the appropriate options in the answer area.
NOTE: Each correct selection is worth one point
A. Mastered
B. Not Mastered
Answer: A

QUESTION 9
- (Exam Topic 3)
You have an Azure virtual network and an on-premises datacenter.
You need to implement a Site-to-Site VPN connection between the datacenter and the virtual network. Which two resources should you create? Each correct
answer presents part of the solution. NOTE: Each
correct selection is worth one point.
A. a virtual network gateway
B. Azure Firewall
C. a local network gateway
D. Azure Web Application Firewall (WAF)
E. an on-premises data gateway
F. an Azure application gateway
G. a user-defined route
Answer: CG

QUESTION 10
- (Exam Topic 3)
You have an Azure subscription that contains the public IP addresses shown in the following table.

You plan to deploy a NAT gateway named NAT1.
Which public IP addresses can be used as the public IP address for NAT1?
A. IP3 and IP5 only
B. IP5 only
C. IP1, IP3, and IP5 only
D. IP3 only
E. IP2 and IP4 only
Answer: D

QUESTION 11
- (Exam Topic 3)
You plan to publish a website that will use an FQDN of www.contoso.com. The website will be hosted by using the Azure App Service apps shown in the following
table.
You plan to use Azure Traffic Manager to manage the routing of traffic for www.contoso.com between AS1 and AS2.

You need to ensure that Traffic Manager routes traffic for www.contoso.com. Which DNS record should you create?
A. two A records that map wmv.contoso.com to 131 107 100 1 and 131 107 200 1
B. a CNAME record that maps www.contoso.com to TMprofile1.azurefd.net
C. a CNAME record that mapswww.contoso.comtoTMprofile1.trafficmanager.net
D. a TXT record that contains a string ofas1.contoso.com and as2.contoso.com in the details
Answer: C

QUESTION 12
- (Exam Topic 3)
You have two Azure virtual networks named Vnet1 and Vnet2 in an Azure region that has three availability zones.
You deploy 12 virtual machines to each virtual network, deploying four virtual machines per zone. The virtual machines in Vnet1 host an app named App1. The
virtual machines in Vnet2 host an app named App2.
You plan to use Azure Virtual Network NAT to implement outbound connectivity for App1 and App2. You need to identify the minimum number of subnets and
Virtual Network NAT instances required to meet
the following requirements:
• A failure of two zones must NOT affect the availability of either App1 or App2.
• A failure of two zones must NOT affect the outbound connectivity of either Appl1or App2. What should you identify? To answer, select the appropriate options in
the answer area. NOTE: Each correct selection is worth one point.
A. Mastered
B. Not Mastered
Answer: A

QUESTION 13
- (Exam Topic 3)
Note: This question is part of a series of questions that present the same scenario. Each question in the series contains a unique solution that might meet stated
goals. Some question sets might have more than one correct solution, while others might not have a correct solution.
After you answer a question in this section, you will NOT be able to return to it. As a result, these questions will not appear in the review screen.
You have an Azure subscription that contains the following resources:
* A virtual network named Vnet1
* A subnet named Subnet1 in Vnet1
* A virtual machine named VM1 that connects to Subnet1
* Three storage accounts named storage1, storage2. and storage3
You need to ensure that VM1 can access storage1. VM1 must be prevented from accessing any other storage accounts.
Solution: You create a network security group (NSG). You configure a service tag for MicrosoftStorage and link the tag to Subnet1.
Does this meet the goal?
A. Yes

B. No
Answer: A

QUESTION 14
- (Exam Topic 3)
Note: This question is part of a series of questions that present the same scenario. Each question in the series contains a unique solution that might meet the
stated goals. Some question sets might have more than one correct solution, while others might not have a correct solution.
After you answer a question in this section, you will NOT be able to return to it. As a result, these questions will not appear in the review screen.
You have an Azure application gateway that has Azure Web Application Firewall (WAF) enabled. You configure the application gateway to direct traffic to the URL
of the application gateway.
You attempt to access the URL and receive an HTTP 403 error. You view the diagnostics log and discover the following error.
You need to ensure that the URL is accessible through the application gateway.
Solution: You create a WAF policy exclusion for request headers that contain 137.135.10.24. Does this meet the goal?
A. Yes
B. No
Answer: B

QUESTION 15
- (Exam Topic 3)
You have an Azure virtual network named Vnet1 that connects to an on-premises network. You have an Azure Storage account named storageaccount1 that
contains blob storage.
You need to configure a private endpoint for the blob storage. The solution must meet the following requirements:

Ensure that all on-premises users can access storageaccount1 through the private endpoint.
Prevent access to storageaccount1 from being interrupted.
Which four actions should you perform in sequence? To answer, move the appropriate actions from the list of actions to the answer area and arrange them in the
correct order.
A. Mastered
B. Not Mastered
Answer: A

QUESTION 16
- (Exam Topic 3)
You have an Azure private DNS zone named contoso.com that is linked to the virtual networks shown in the following table.
The links have auto registration enabled.
You create the virtual machines shown in the following table.

You manually add the following entry to the contoso.com zone:
Name: VM1
IP address: 10.1.10.9
For each of the following statements, select Yes of the statement is true. Otherwise, select No. NOTE: Each correct selection is worth one point.
A. Mastered
B. Not Mastered
Answer: A

QUESTION 17
- (Exam Topic 3)
You have an Azure subscription that contains a single virtual network and a virtual network gateway.
You need to ensure that administrators can use Point-to-Site (P2S) VPN connections to access resources in the virtual network. The connections must be
authenticated by Azure Active Directory (Azure AD).
What should you configure? To answer, select the appropriate options in the answer area. NOTE: Each correct selection is worth one point.
A. Mastered
B. Not Mastered
Answer: A

QUESTION 18
- (Exam Topic 3)
Note: This question is part of a series of questions that present the same scenario. Each question in the series contains a unique solution that might meet the
stated goals. Some question sets might have more than one correct solution, while others might not have a correct solution.
After you answer a question in this section, you will NOT be able to return to it. As a result, these questions will not appear in the review screen.
You have an Azure subscription that contains the following resources:
* A virtual network named Vnet1
* A subnet named Subnet1 in Vnet1
* A virtual machine named VM1 that connects to Subnet1
* Three storage accounts named storage1, storage2, and storage3
You need to ensure that VM1 can access storage1. VM1 must be prevented from accessing any other storage accounts.
Solution: You create a network security group (NSG) and associate the NSG to Subnet1. Does this meet the goal?
A. Yes
B. No
Answer: A

QUESTION 19
- (Exam Topic 3)

Note: This question is part of a series of questions that present the same scenario. Each question in the series contains a unique solution that might meet the stated goals. Some question sets might have more than one correct solution, while others might not have a correct solution.

After you answer a question in this section, you will NOT be able to return to it. As a result, these questions will not appear in the review screen.

You have an Azure application gateway that has Azure Web Application Firewall (WAF) enabled. You configure the application gateway to direct traffic to the URL of the application gateway.

You attempt to access the URL and receive an HTTP 403 error. You view the diagnostics log and discover the following error.

You need to ensure that the URL is accessible through the application gateway. Solution: You configure a custom cookie and an exclusion rule.

Does this meet the goal?

A. Yes

B. No

Answer: A

QUESTION 20

- (Exam Topic 3)

Note: This question is part of a series of questions that present the same scenario. Each question in the series contains a unique solution that might meet the stated goals. Some question sets might have more than one correct solution, while others might not have a correct solution.

After you answer a question in this section, you will NOT be able to return to it. As a result, these questions will not appear in the review screen.

You have two Azure virtual networks named Vnet1 and Vnet2.

You have a Windows 10 device named Client1 that connects to Vnet1 by using a Point-to-Site (P2S) IKEv2 VPN.

You implement virtual network peering between Vnet1 and Vnet2. Vnet1 allows gateway transit. Vnet2 can use the remote gateway.

You discover that Client1 cannot communicate with Vnet2. You need to ensure that Client1 can communicate with Vnet2.

Solution: You download and reinstall the VPN client configuration. Does this meet the goal?

A. Yes

B. No

Answer: A

QUESTION 21

- (Exam Topic 3)

You have an Azure firewall shown in the following exhibit.

Use the drop-down menus to select the answer choice that completes each statement based on the information presented in the graphic.

NOTE: Each correct selection is worth one point.

A. Mastered
B. Not Mastered
Answer: A
QUESTION 22
- (Exam Topic 3)
You have five virtual machines that run Windows Server. Each virtual machine hosts a different web app. You plan to use an Azure application gateway to provide
access to each web app by using a hostname of
www.contoso.corn and a different URL path for each web app, for example: https://www.contoso.com/app1.
You need to control the flow of traffic based on the URL path. What should you configure?

A. rules
B. rewrites
C. HTTP settings
D. listeners
Answer: A

QUESTION 23
- (Exam Topic 1)
You need to prepare Vnet1 for the deployment of an ExpressRoute gateway. The solution must meet the hybrid connectivity requirements and the business
requirements.
Which three actions should you perform in sequence for Vnet1? To answer, move the appropriate actions from the list of actions to the answer area and arrange
them in the correct order.
A. Mastered
B. Not Mastered
Answer: A

QUESTION 24
- (Exam Topic 1)
You need to restrict traffic from VMScaleSet1 to VMScaleSet2. The solution must meet the virtual networking requirements.
What is the minimum number of custom NSG rules and NSG assignments required? To answer, select the appropriate options in the answer area.
NOTE: Each correct selection is worth one point.
A. Mastered
B. Not Mastered
Answer: A

QUESTION 25
- (Exam Topic 1)
You need to implement a P2S VPN for the users in the branch office. The solution must meet the hybrid networking requirements.

What should you do? To answer, select the appropriate options in the answer area. NOTE: Each correct selection is worth one point.
A. Mastered
B. Not Mastered
Answer: A

QUESTION 26
- (Exam Topic 1)
You need to recommend a configuration for the ExpressRoute connection from the Boston datacenter. The solution must meet the hybrid networking requirements
and business requirements.
What should you recommend? To answer, select the appropriate options in the answer area. NOTE: Each correct selection is worth one point.
A. Mastered
B. Not Mastered
Answer: A

QUESTION 27
- (Exam Topic 2)
You need to configure GW1 to meet the network security requirements for the P2S VPN users. Which Tunnel type should you select in the Point-to-site
configuration settings of GW1?
A. IKEv2 and OpenVPN (SSL)
B. IKEv2
C. IKEv2 and SSTP (SSL)
D. OpenVPN (SSL)
E. SSTP (SSL)
Answer: D

QUESTION 28
- (Exam Topic 2)
You are implementing the virtual network requirements for VM Analyze.
What should you include in a custom route that is linked to Subnet2? To answer, select the appropriate options in the answer area.
NOTE: Each correct selection is worth one point.
A. Mastered
B. Not Mastered
Answer: A

QUESTION 29
- (Exam Topic 3)
Note: This question is part of a series of questions that present the same scenario. Each question in the series contains a unique solution that might meet the
stated goals. Some question sets might have more than one correct solution, while others might not have a correct solution.

After you answer a question in this section, you will NOT be able to return to it. As a result, these questions will not appear in the review screen.
You have two Azure virtual networks named Vnet1 and Vnet2.
You have a Windows 10 device named Client1 that connects to Vnet1 by using a Point-to-Site (P2S) IKEv2 VPN.
You implement virtual network peering between Vnet1 and Vnet2. Vnet1 allows gateway transit. Vnet2 can use the remote gateway.
You discover that Client1 cannot communicate with Vnet2. You need to ensure that Client1 can communicate with Vnet2. Solution: You reset the gateway of
Vnet1.
Does this meet the goal?
A. Yes
B. No
Answer: B

QUESTION 30
- (Exam Topic 3)
You are planning the IP addressing for the subnets in Azure virtual networks. Which type of resource requires IP addresses in the subnets?
A. Azure Virtual Network NAT
B. virtual network peering
C. service endpoints
D. private endpoints
Answer: A

QUESTION 31
- (Exam Topic 3)
You have an Azure virtual network named Vnet1 that has one subnet. Vnet1 is in the West Europe Azure region.
You deploy an Azure App Service app named App1 to the West Europe region.
You need to provide App1 with access to the resources in Vnet1. The solution must minimize costs. What should you do first?
A. Create a private link.
B. Create a new subnet.
C. Create a NAT gateway.
D. Create a gateway subnet and deploy a virtual network gateway.
Answer: B
QUESTION 32
- (Exam Topic 3)
You have two Azure subscriptions named Subscnption1 and Subscription2. Subscription1 contains a virtual network named Vnet1. Vnet1 contains an application
server. Subscription2 contains a virtual network named Vnet2.
You need to provide the virtual machines in Vnet2 with access to the application server in Vnet1 by using a private endpoint.
Which four actions should you perform in sequence? To answer, move the appropriate actions from the list of actions to the answer area and arrange them in the

correct order.
A. Mastered
B. Not Mastered
Answer: A

QUESTION 33
- (Exam Topic 3)
You plan to deploy an Azure virtual network. You need to design the subnets.
Which three types of resources require a dedicated subnet? Each correct answer presents a complete solution. NOTE: Each correct selection is worth one point.
A. VPN gateway
B. Azure Bastion
C. Azure Active Directory Domain Services (Azure AD DS)
D. Azure Application Gateway v2
E. Azure Private Link
Answer: ABD

QUESTION 14
- (Exam Topic 3)
You have Azure App Service apps in the West US Azure region as shown in the following table.
You need to ensure that all the apps can access the resources in a virtual network named Vnet1 without forwarding traffic through the internet-How many
integration subnets should you create?
A. 1
B. 3
C. 4
D. 6
Answer: D

QUESTION 15
- (Exam Topic 3)
You have an Azure virtual network named Vnet1.
You need to ensure that the virtual machines in Vnet1 can access only the Azure SQL resources in the East US Azure region. The virtual machines must be
prevented from accessing any Azure Storage resources.
Which two outbound network security group (NSG) rules should you create? Each correct answer presents part of the solution.
NOTE: Each correct selection is worth one point.
A. an allow rule that has the IP address range of Vnet1 as the source and destination of Sql.EastUS
B. a deny rule that has a source of VirtualNetwork and a destination of Sql
C. a deny rule that has a source of VirtualNetwork and a destination of 168.63.129.0/24
D. a deny rule that has the IP address range of Vnet1 as the source and destination of Storage
Answer: CD

QUESTION 16
- (Exam Topic 3)

You have an Azure subscription that contains the resources shown in the following table.
The IP Addresses settings for Vnet1 are configured as shown in the exhibit.
You need to ensure that you can integrate WebApp1 and Vnet1.
Which three actions should you perform in sequence before you can integrate WebApp1 and Vnet1? To answer, move the appropriate actions from the list of actions to the answer area and arrange them in the correct order.
A. Mastered
B. Not Mastered
Answer: A

QUESTION 17
- (Exam Topic 3)
You have the Azure Traffic Manager profiles shown in the following table.
You plan to add the endpoints shown in the following table.
Which endpoints can you add to Profile2?
A. Endpoint1 and Endpoint4 only
B. Endpoint1, Endpoint2, Endpoint3, and Endpoint4
C. Endpoint1 only
D. Endpoint2 and Endpoint3 only
E. Endpoint3 only
Answer: A

QUESTION 18
- (Exam Topic 3)
Azure virtual networks in the East US Azure region as shown in the following table.
The virtual networks are peered to one another. Each virtual network contains four subnets.
You plan to deploy a virtual machine named VM1 that will inspect and route traffic between all the subnets on both the virtual networks.
What is the minimum number of IP addresses that you must assign to VM1?
A. 1
B. 2
C. 4
D. 8
Answer: A

QUESTION 19
- (Exam Topic 3)
Note: This question is part of a series of questions that present the same scenario. Each question in the series contains a unique solution that might meet the stated goals. Some question sets might have more than one correct solution, while others might not have a correct solution.
After you answer a question in this section, you will NOT be able to return to it. As a result, these questions will not appear in the review screen.
You have an Azure application gateway that has Azure Web Application Firewall (WAF) enabled.
You configure the application gateway to direct traffic to the URL of the application gateway.

You attempt to access the URL and receive an HTTP 403 error. You view the diagnostics log and discover the following error.
You need to ensure that the URL is accessible through the application gateway.
Solution: You create a WAF policy exclusion for request headers that contain 137.135.10.24. Does this meet the goal?
A. Yes
B. No
Answer: B

QUESTION 20
- (Exam Topic 3)
Note: This question is part of a series of questions that present the same scenario. Each question in the series contains a unique solution that might meet the
stated goals. Some question sets might have more than one correct solution, while others might not have a correct solution.
After you answer a question in this section, you will NOT be able to return to it. As a result, these questions will not appear in the review screen.
You have an Azure subscription that contains the following resources:
* A virtual network named Vnet1
* A subnet named Subnet1 in Vnet1
* A virtual machine named VM1 that connects to Subnet1
* Three storage accounts named storage1, storage2, and storage3
You need to ensure that VM1 can access storage1. VM1 must be prevented from accessing any other storage accounts.
Solution: You configure the firewall on storage1 to only accept connections from Vnet1. Does this meet the goal?
A. Yes
B. No
Answer: B

QUESTION 21
- (Exam Topic 3)
You have an Azure virtual network named Vnet1 that connects to an on-premises network. You have an Azure Storage account named storageaccount1 that
contains blob storage.
You need to configure a private endpoint for the blob storage. The solution must meet the following requirements:
Ensure that all on-premises users can access storageaccount1 through the private endpoint.
Prevent access to storageaccount1 from being interrupted.
Which four actions should you perform in sequence
A. Mastered
B. Not Mastered
Answer: A

QUESTION 22
- (Exam Topic 3)

You have an Azure subscription that contains the following resources:
A virtual network named Vnet1
Two subnets named subnet1 and AzureFirewallSubnet
A public Azure Firewall named FW1
A route table named RT1 that is associated to Subnet1
A rule routing of 0.0.0.0/0 to FW1 in RT1
After deploying 10 servers that run Windows Server to Subnet1, you discover that none of the virtual machines were activated.
You need to ensure that the virtual machines can be activated. What should you do?
A. On FW1, create an outbound service tag rule for AzureCloud.
B. On FW1, create an outbound network rule that allows traffic to the Azure Key Management Service (KMS).
C. Deploy a NAT gateway.
D. To Subnetl, associate a network security group (NSG) that allows outbound access to port 1688.
Answer: B

QUESTION 23
- (Exam Topic 3)
You are configuring two network virtual appliances (NVAs) in an Azure virtual network. The NVAs will be used to inspect all the traffic within the virtual network.
You need to provide high availability for the NVAs. The solution must minimize administrative effort. What should you include in the solution?
A. Azure Standard Load Balancer
B. Azure Traffic Manager
C. Azure Application Gateway
D. Azure Front Door
Answer: A

QUESTION 24
- (Exam Topic 3)
You have an Azure subscription that contains a single virtual network and a virtual network gateway.
You need to ensure that administrators can use Point-to-Site (P2S) VPN connections to access resources in the virtual network. The connections must be
authenticated by Azure Active Directory (Azure AD).
What should you configure? To answer, select the appropriate options in the answer area. NOTE: Each correct selection is worth one point.
A. Mastered
B. Not Mastered
Answer: A

QUESTION 25
- (Exam Topic 3)
You have an Azure application gateway named AGW1 that
has a routing rule named Rule1. Rule 1 directs traffic for http://www.contoso.com to a backend pool named Pool1. Pool1 targets an Azure virtual machine scale set

named VMSS1.
You deploy another virtual machine scale set named VMSS2. You need to configure AGW1 to direct all traffic for http://www.adatum.com to VMSS2.
The solution must ensure that requests to http://www.contoso.com continue to be directed to Pool1.
Which three actions should you perform? Each correct answer presents part of the solution. NOTE: Each correct selection is worth one point.
A. Add a backend pool.
B. Modify an HTTP setting.
C. Add an HTTP setting.
D. Add a listener.
E. Add a rule.
Answer: ADE

QUESTION 26
- (Exam Topic 3)
You have the Azure resources shown in the following table.
You configure storage1 to provide access to the subnet in Vnet1 by using a service endpoint.
You need to ensure that you can use the service endpoint to connect to the read-only endpoint of storage1 in the paired Azure region.
What should you do first?
A. Configure the firewall settings for storage1.
B. Fail over storage1 to the paired Azure region.
C. Create a virtual network in the paired Azure region.
D. Create another service endpoint.
Answer: A

QUESTION 27
- (Exam Topic 3)
Your company has 10 instances of a web service. Each instance is hosted in a different Azure region and is accessible through a public endpoint.
The development department at the company is creating an application named App1. Every 10 minutes. App1 will use a list of end points and connect to the first available endpoint.
You plan to use Azure Traffic Manager to maintain the list of endpoints.
You need to configure a Traffic Manager profile that will minimize the impact of DNS caching.
What should you configure?
A. Mastered
B. Not Mastered
Answer: A

QUESTION 28
- (Exam Topic 3)
Note: This question is part of a series of questions that present the same scenario. Each question in the series contains a unique solution that might meet the stated goals. Some question sets might have more than one correct solution, while others might not have a correct solution.

After you answer a question in this section, you will NOT be able to return to it. As a result, these questions will not appear in the review screen.
You have an Azure subscription that contains the following resources:
* A virtual network named Vnet1
* A subnet named Subnet1 in Vnet1
* A virtual machine named VM1 that connects to Subnet1
* Three storage accounts named storage1, storage2, and storage3
You need to ensure that VM1 can access storage1. VM1 must be prevented from accessing any other storage accounts.
Solution: You create a network security group (NSG) and associate the NSG to Subnet1. Does this meet the goal?
A. Yes
B. No
Answer: A

QUESTION 29
- (Exam Topic 3)
You plan to configure BGP for a Site-to-Site VPN connection between a datacenter and Azure. Which two Azure resources should you configure? Each correct
answer presents a part of the solution.
(Choose two.)
NOTE: Each correct selection is worth one point.
A. a virtual network gateway
B. Azure Application Gateway
C. Azure Firewall
D. a local network gateway
E. Azure Front Door
Answer: AD

QUESTION 30
- (Exam Topic 3)
Your company has an Azure virtual network named Vnet1 that uses an IP address space of 192.168.0.0/20. Vnet1 contains a subnet named Subnet1 that uses an
IP address space of 192.168.0.0/24.
You create an IPv6 address range to Vnet1 by using a CIDR suffix of /48.
You need to enable the virtual machines on Subnet1 to communicate with each other by using IPv6 addresses assigned by the company. The solution must
minimize the number of additional IPv4 addresses.
What should you do?
A. Mastered
B. Not Mastered
Answer: A

QUESTION 31
- (Exam Topic 3)

Your company has offices in New York and Amsterdam. The company has an Azure subscription. Both offices connect to Azure by using a Site-to-Site VPN
connection.
The office in Amsterdam uses resources in the North Europe Azure region. The office in New York uses resources in the East US Azure region.
You need to implement ExpressRoute circuits to connect each office to the nearest Azure region. Once the ExpressRoute circuits are connected, the on-premises
computers in the Amsterdam office must be able to connect to the on-premises servers in the New York office by using the ExpressRoute circuits.
Which ExpressRoute option should you use?
A. ExpressRoute Local
B. ExpressRoute FastPath
C. ExpressRoute Direct
D. ExpressRoute Global Reach
Answer: A

QUESTION 32
- (Exam Topic 3)
You have an Azure virtual network that contains two subnets named Subnet1 and Subnet2. Subnet1 contains a virtual machine named VM1. Subnet2 contains a
virtual machine named VM2.
You have two network security groups (NSGs) named NSG1 and NSG2. NSG1 has 100 inbound security rules and is associated to VM1. NSG2 has 200 inbound
security rules and is associated to Subnet1.
VM2 cannot connect to VM1.
You suspect that an NSG rule blocks connectivity.
You need to identify which rule blocks the connection. The issue must be resolved as quickly as possible. Which Azure Network Watcher feature should you use?
A. Effective security rules
B. Connection troubleshoot
C. NSG diagnostic
D. NSG flow logs
Answer: C

QUESTION 33
- (Exam Topic 3)
You fail to establish a Site-to-Site VPN connection between your company's main office and an Azure virtual network.
You need to troubleshoot what prevents you from establishing the IPsec tunnel. Which diagnostic log should you review?
A. IKEDiagnosticLog
B. GatewayDiagnosticLog
C. TunnelDiagnosticLog
D. RouteDiagnosticLog
Answer: A

QUESTION 34

- (Exam Topic 3)

Your company has an on-premises network and three Azure subscriptions named Subscription1, Subscription2, and Subscription3.

The departments at the company use the Azure subscriptions as shown in the following table.

All the resources in the subscriptions are in either the West US Azure region or the West US 2 Azure region. You plan to connect all the subscriptions to the onpremises network by using ExpressRoute.

What is the minimum number of ExpressRoute circuits required?

A. 1

B. 2

C. 3

D. 4

E. 5

Answer: A

QUESTION 35

- (Exam Topic 3)

You have an Azure subscription that contains multiple virtual machines in the West US Azure region. You need to use Traffic Analytics.

Which two resources should you create? Each correct answer presents part of the solution. (Choose two.) NOTE: Each correct answer selection is worth one point.

A. an Azure Monitor workbook

B. a Log Analytics workspace C a storage account

C. an Azure Sentinel workspace

D. an Azure Monitor data collection rule

Answer: BC

QUESTION 36

- (Exam Topic 3)

You have an Azure subscription that contains two virtual networks named Vnet1 and Vnet2.

You register a public DNS zone named fabrikam.com. The zone is configured as shown in the Public DNS Zone exhibit.

For each of the following statements, select Yes if the statement is true. Otherwise, select No. NOTE: Each correct selection is worth one point.

A. Mastered

B. Not Mastered

Answer: A

QUESTION 37

- (Exam Topic 3)

You have an Azure Front Door instance named FrontDoor1.

You deploy two instances of an Azure web app to different Azure regions.

You plan to provide access to the web app through FrontDoor1 by using the name app1.contoso.com. You need to ensure that FrontDoor1 is the entry point for

requests that use app1.contoso.com.
Which three actions should you perform in sequence? To answer, move the appropriate actions from the list of actions to the answer area and arrange them in the
correct order.
A. Mastered
B. Not Mastered
Answer: A

QUESTION 38
- (Exam Topic 3)
Note: This question is part of a series of questions that present the same scenario. Each question in the series contains a unique solution that might meet the
stated goals. Some question sets might have more than one correct solution, while others might not have a correct solution.
After you answer a question in this section, you will NOT be able to return to it. As a result, these questions will not appear in the review screen.
You have an Azure application gateway that has Azure Web Application Firewall (WAF) enabled. You configure the application gateway to direct traffic to the URL
of the application gateway.
You attempt to access the URL and receive an HTTP 403 error. You view the diagnostics log and discover the following error.
You need to ensure that the URL is accessible through the application gateway. Solution: You add a rewrite rule for the host header.
Does this meet the goal?
A. Yes
B. No
Answer: B

QUESTION 39
- (Exam Topic 3)
You have an Azure subscription that contains an Azure App Service app. The app uses a URL of https://www.contoso.com.
You need to use a custom domain on Azure Front Door for www.contoso.com. The custom domain must use a certificate from an allowed certification authority
(CA).
What should you include in the solution?
A. an enterprise application in Azure Active Directory (Azure AD)
B. Active Directory Certificate Services (AD CS)
C. Azure Key Vault
D. Azure Application Gateway
Answer: C

QUESTION 40
- (Exam Topic 3)
You have five virtual machines that run Windows Server. Each virtual machine hosts a different web app. You plan to use an Azure application gateway to provide

access to each web app by using a hostname of
www.contoso.corn and a different URL path for each web app, for example: https://www.contoso.com/app1.
You need to control the flow of traffic based on the URL path. What should you configure?
A. rules
B. rewrites
C. HTTP settings
D. listeners
Answer: A

QUESTION 41
- (Exam Topic 1)
You need to provide connectivity to storage1. The solution must meet the PaaS networking requirements and the business requirements.
What should you include in the solution?
A. a service endpoint
B. Azure Front Door
C. a private endpoint
D. Azure Traffic Manager
Answer: A

QUESTION 42
- (Exam Topic 2)
You create NSG10 and NSG11 to meet the network security requirements.
For each of the following statements, select Yes it the statement is true. Otherwise, select No.
NOTE: Each correct selection is worth one point.
A. Mastered
B. Not Mastered
Answer: A

QUESTION 43
- (Exam Topic 2)
What should you implement to meet the virtual network requirements for the virtual machines that connect to Vnet4 and Vnet5?
A. a private endpoint
B. a virtual network peering
C. a private link service
D. a routing table
E. a service endpoint
Answer: B

QUESTION 45
- (Exam Topic 3)
You have 10 Azure App Service instances. Each instance hosts the same web app. Each instance is in a different Azure region.

You need to configure Azure Traffic Manager to direct users to the instance that has the lowest latency. Which routing method should you use?
A. geographic
B. weighted
C. performance
D. priority
Answer: D

QUESTION 46
- (Exam Topic 3)
You have an Azure Front Door instance named FD1 that is protected by using Azure Web Application Firewall (WAF).
FD1 uses a frontend host named app1.contoso.com to provide access to Azure web apps hosted in the East US Azure region and the West US Azure region.
You need to configure FD1 to block requests to app1.contoso.com from all countries other than the United States.
What should you include in the WAF policy?
A. a frontend host association
B. a managed rule set
C. a custom rule that uses a rate limit rule
D. a custom rule that uses a match rule
Answer: C

QUESTION 47
- (Exam Topic 3)
You are planning the IP addressing for the subnets in Azure virtual networks. Which type of resource requires IP addresses in the subnets?
A. Azure Virtual Network NAT
B. virtual network peering
C. service endpoints
D. private endpoints
Answer: A
QUESTION 48
- (Exam Topic 3)
You have an Azure virtual network named Vnet1 that has one subnet. Vnet1 is in the West Europe Azure region.
You deploy an Azure App Service app named App1 to the West Europe region.
You need to provide App1 with access to the resources in Vnet1. The solution must minimize costs. What should you do first?
A. Create a private link.
B. Create a new subnet.
C. Create a NAT gateway.
D. Create a gateway subnet and deploy a virtual network gateway.
Answer: B
.920
QUESTION 49

- (Exam Topic 3)
You have an Azure Traffic Manager parent profile named TM1. TM1 has two child profiles named TM2 and TM3.
TM1 uses the performance traffic-routing method and has the endpoints shown in the following table.
TM2 uses the weighted traffic-routing method with MinChildEndpoint = 2 and has the endpoints shown in the following table.
TM3 uses priority traffic-routing method and has the endpoints shown in the following table.
The App2, App4, and App6 endpoints have a degraded monitoring status.
To which endpoint is traffic directed? To answer, select the appropriate options in the answer area.
NOTE: Each correct selection is worth one point
A. Mastered
B. Not Mastered
Answer: A

QUESTION 50
- (Exam Topic 3)
You have an Azure virtual network and an on-premises datacenter.
You need to implement a Site-to-Site VPN connection between the datacenter and the virtual network. Which two resources should you create? Each correct
answer presents part of the solution. NOTE: Each
correct selection is worth one point.
A. a virtual network gateway
B. Azure Firewall
C. a local network gateway
D. Azure Web Application Firewall (WAF)
E. an on-premises data gateway
F. an Azure application gateway
G. a user-defined route
Answer: CG

QUESTION 51
- (Exam Topic 3)
You have an Azure subscription that contains the public IP addresses shown in the following table.
You plan to deploy a NAT gateway named NAT1.
Which public IP addresses can be used as the public IP address for NAT1?
A. IP3 and IP5 only
B. IP5 only
C. IP1, IP3, and IP5 only
D. IP3 only
E. IP2 and IP4 only
Answer: D

QUESTION 52
- (Exam Topic 3)

You plan to publish a website that will use an FQDN of www.contoso.com. The website will be hosted by using the Azure App Service apps shown in the following
table.
You plan to use Azure Traffic Manager to manage the routing of traffic for www.contoso.com between AS1 and AS2.
You need to ensure that Traffic Manager routes traffic for www.contoso.com. Which DNS record should you create?
A. two A records that map wmv.contoso.com to 131 107 100 1 and 131 107 200 1
B. a CNAME record that maps www.contoso.com to TMprofile1.azurefd.net
C. a CNAME record that mapswww.contoso.comtoTMprofile1.trafficmanager.net
D. a TXT record that contains a string ofas1.contoso.com and as2.contoso.com in the details
Answer: C

QUESTION 53

- (Exam Topic 3)
You have two Azure virtual networks named Vnet1 and Vnet2 in an Azure region that has three availability zones.
You deploy 12 virtual machines to each virtual network, deploying four virtual machines per zone. The virtual machines in Vnet1 host an app named App1. The
virtual machines in Vnet2 host an app named App2.
You plan to use Azure Virtual Network NAT to implement outbound connectivity for App1 and App2. You need to identify the minimum number of subnets and
Virtual Network NAT instances required to meet
the following requirements:
• A failure of two zones must NOT affect the availability of either App1 or App2.
• A failure of two zones must NOT affect the outbound connectivity of either Appl1or App2. What should you identify? To answer, select the appropriate options in
the answer area. NOTE: Each correct selection is worth one point.
A. Mastered
B. Not Mastered
Answer: A

QUESTION 54

- (Exam Topic 3)
Note: This question is part of a series of questions that present the same scenario. Each question in the series contains a unique solution that might meet stated
goals. Some question sets might have more than one correct solution, while others might not have a correct solution.
After you answer a question in this section, you will NOT be able to return to it. As a result, these questions will not appear in the review screen.
You have an Azure subscription that contains the following resources:
* A virtual network named Vnet1
* A subnet named Subnet1 in Vnet1
* A virtual machine named VM1 that connects to Subnet1
* Three storage accounts named storage1, storage2. and storage3

You need to ensure that VM1 can access storage1. VM1 must be prevented from accessing any other storage accounts.
Solution: You create a network security group (NSG). You configure a service tag for MicrosoftStorage and link the tag to Subnet1.
Does this meet the goal?
A. Yes
B. No
Answer: A

QUESTION 55
- (Exam Topic 3)
Note: This question is part of a series of questions that present the same scenario. Each question in the series contains a unique solution that might meet the
stated goals. Some question sets might have more than one correct solution, while others might not have a correct solution.
After you answer a question in this section, you will NOT be able to return to it. As a result, these questions will not appear in the review screen.
You have an Azure application gateway that has Azure Web Application Firewall (WAF) enabled. You configure the application gateway to direct traffic to the URL
of the application gateway.
You attempt to access the URL and receive an HTTP 403 error. You view the diagnostics log and discover the following error.
You need to ensure that the URL is accessible through the application gateway.
Solution: You create a WAF policy exclusion for request headers that contain 137.135.10.24. Does this meet the goal?
A. Yes
B. No
Answer: B

QUESTION 56
- (Exam Topic 3)
You have an Azure virtual network named Vnet1 that connects to an on-premises network. You have an Azure Storage account named storageaccount1 that
contains blob storage.
You need to configure a private endpoint for the blob storage. The solution must meet the following requirements:
Ensure that all on-premises users can access storageaccount1 through the private endpoint.
Prevent access to storageaccount1 from being interrupted.
Which four actions should you perform in sequence? To answer, move the appropriate actions from the list of actions to the answer area and arrange them in the
correct order.
A. Mastered
B. Not Mastered
Answer: A

QUESTION 57

- (Exam Topic 3)
You have an Azure private DNS zone named contoso.com that is linked to the virtual networks shown in the following table.
The links have auto registration enabled.
You create the virtual machines shown in the following table.
You manually add the following entry to the contoso.com zone:
Name: VM1
IP address: 10.1.10.9
For each of the following statements, select Yes of the statement is true. Otherwise, select No.
NOTE: Each correct selection is worth one point.
A. Mastered
B. Not Mastered
Answer: A

QUESTION 58
- (Exam Topic 3)
You have an Azure subscription that contains a single virtual network and a virtual network gateway.
You need to ensure that administrators can use Point-to-Site (P2S) VPN connections to access resources in the virtual network. The connections must be authenticated by Azure Active Directory (Azure AD).
What should you configure?
A. Mastered
B. Not Mastered
Answer: A

QUESTION 59
- (Exam Topic 3)
Note: This question is part of a series of questions that present the same scenario. Each question in the series contains a unique solution that might meet the stated goals. Some question sets might have more than one correct solution, while others might not have a correct solution.
After you answer a question in this section, you will NOT be able to return to it. As a result, these questions will not appear in the review screen.
You have an Azure subscription that contains the following resources:
* A virtual network named Vnet1
* A subnet named Subnet1 in Vnet1
* A virtual machine named VM1 that connects to Subnet1
* Three storage accounts named storage1, storage2, and storage3
You need to ensure that VM1 can access storage1. VM1 must be prevented from accessing any other storage accounts.
Solution: You create a network security group (NSG) and associate the NSG to Subnet1. Does this meet the goal?
A. Yes
B. No
Answer: A

QUESTION 60

- (Exam Topic 3)

Note: This question is part of a series of questions that present the same scenario. Each question in the series contains a unique solution that might meet the
stated goals. Some question sets might have more than one correct solution, while others might not have a correct solution.
After you answer a question in this section, you will NOT be able to return to it. As a result, these questions will not appear in the review screen.
You have an Azure application gateway that has Azure Web Application Firewall (WAF) enabled. You configure the application gateway to direct traffic to the URL
of the application gateway.
You attempt to access the URL and receive an HTTP 403 error. You view the diagnostics log and discover the following error.

You need to ensure that the URL is accessible through the application gateway. Solution: You configure a custom cookie and an exclusion rule.
Does this meet the goal?
A. Yes
B. No
Answer: A

QUESTION 61

- (Exam Topic 3)

Note: This question is part of a series of questions that present the same scenario. Each question in the series contains a unique solution that might meet the
stated goals. Some question sets might have more than one correct solution, while others might not have a correct solution.
After you answer a question in this section, you will NOT be able to return to it. As a result, these questions will not appear in the review screen.
You have two Azure virtual networks named Vnet1 and Vnet2.
You have a Windows 10 device named Client1 that connects to Vnet1 by using a Point-to-Site (P2S) IKEv2 VPN.
You implement virtual network peering between Vnet1 and Vnet2. Vnet1 allows gateway transit. Vnet2 can use the remote gateway.
You discover that Client1 cannot communicate with Vnet2. You need to ensure that Client1 can communicate with Vnet2.
Solution: You download and reinstall the VPN client configuration. Does this meet the goal?
A. Yes
B. No
Answer: A

QUESTION 62

- (Exam Topic 3)

You have an Azure firewall shown in the following exhibit.
Use the drop-down menus to select the answer choice that completes each statement based on the information presented in the graphic.

NOTE: Each correct selection is worth one point.
A. Mastered
B. Not Mastered
Answer: A

QUESTION 63
- (Exam Topic 3)
You have five virtual machines that run Windows Server. Each virtual machine hosts a different web app. You plan to use an Azure application gateway to provide
access to each web app by using a hostname of
www.contoso.corn and a different URL path for each web app, for example: https://www.contoso.com/app1.
You need to control the flow of traffic based on the URL path. What should you configure?
A. rules
B. rewrites
C. HTTP settings
D. listeners
Answer: A

QUESTION 64
- (Exam Topic 1)
You need to provide connectivity to storage1. The solution must meet the PaaS networking requirements and the business requirements.
What should you include in the solution?
A. a service endpoint
B. Azure Front Door
C. a private endpoint
D. Azure Traffic Manager
Answer: A

QUESTION 65
- (Exam Topic 3)
You have 10 Azure App Service instances. Each instance hosts the same web app. Each instance is in a different Azure region.
You need to configure Azure Traffic Manager to direct users to the instance that has the lowest latency. Which routing method should you use?
A. geographic
B. weighted
C. performance
D. priority
Answer: D

QUESTION 66
- (Exam Topic 3)
You have an Azure Front Door instance named FD1 that is protected by using Azure Web Application Firewall (WAF).

FD1 uses a frontend host named app1.contoso.com to provide access to Azure web apps hosted in the East US Azure region and the West US Azure region.
You need to configure FD1 to block requests to app1.contoso.com from all countries other than the United States.
What should you include in the WAF policy?
A. a frontend host association
B. a managed rule set
C. a custom rule that uses a rate limit rule
D. a custom rule that uses a match rule
Answer: C

QUESTION 67
- (Exam Topic 3)
You are planning the IP addressing for the subnets in Azure virtual networks. Which type of resource requires IP addresses in the subnets?
A. Azure Virtual Network NAT
B. virtual network peering
C. service endpoints
D. private endpoints
Answer: A

QUESTION 68
- (Exam Topic 3)
You have an Azure virtual network named Vnet1 that has one subnet. Vnet1 is in the West Europe Azure region.
You deploy an Azure App Service app named App1 to the West Europe region.
You need to provide App1 with access to the resources in Vnet1. The solution must minimize costs. What should you do first?
A. Create a private link.
B. Create a new subnet.
C. Create a NAT gateway.
D. Create a gateway subnet and deploy a virtual network gateway.
Answer: B

QUESTION 69
- (Exam Topic 3)
You have an Azure Traffic Manager parent profile named TM1. TM1 has two child profiles named TM2 and TM3.
TM1 uses the performance traffic-routing method and has the endpoints shown in the following table.
TM2 uses the weighted traffic-routing method with MinChildEndpoint = 2 and has the endpoints shown in the following table.
TM3 uses priority traffic-routing method and has the endpoints shown in the following table.
The App2, App4, and App6 endpoints have a degraded monitoring status.
To which endpoint is traffic directed? To answer, select the appropriate options in the answer area.
NOTE: Each correct selection is worth one point

A. Mastered
B. Not Mastered
Answer: A

QUESTION 70
- (Exam Topic 3)
You have an Azure virtual network and an on-premises datacenter.
You need to implement a Site-to-Site VPN connection between the datacenter and the virtual network. Which two resources should you create? Each correct answer presents part of the solution. NOTE: Each correct selection is worth one point.
A. a virtual network gateway
B. Azure Firewall
C. a local network gateway
D. Azure Web Application Firewall (WAF)
E. an on-premises data gateway
F. an Azure application gateway
G. a user-defined route
Answer: CG

QUESTION 71
- (Exam Topic 3)
You have an Azure subscription that contains the public IP addresses shown in the following table.
You plan to deploy a NAT gateway named NAT1.
Which public IP addresses can be used as the public IP address for NAT1?
A. IP3 and IP5 only
B. IP5 only
C. IP1, IP3, and IP5 only
D. IP3 only
E. IP2 and IP4 only
Answer: D

QUESTION 72
- (Exam Topic 3)
You plan to publish a website that will use an FQDN of www.contoso.com. The website will be hosted by using the Azure App Service apps shown in the following table.
You plan to use Azure Traffic Manager to manage the routing of traffic for www.contoso.com between AS1 and AS2.
You need to ensure that Traffic Manager routes traffic for www.contoso.com. Which DNS record should you create?
A. two A records that map wmv.contoso.com to 131 107 100 1 and 131 107 200 1
B. a CNAME record that maps www.contoso.com to TMprofile1.azurefd.net
C. a CNAME record that mapswww.contoso.comtoTMprofile1.trafficmanager.net
D. a TXT record that contains a string ofas1.contoso.com and as2.contoso.com in the details
Answer: C

QUESTION 73
- (Exam Topic 3)
You have two Azure virtual networks named Vnet1 and Vnet2 in an Azure region that has three availability zones.
You deploy 12 virtual machines to each virtual network, deploying four virtual machines per zone. The virtual machines in Vnet1 host an app named App1. The
virtual machines in Vnet2 host an app named App2.
You plan to use Azure Virtual Network NAT to implement outbound connectivity for App1 and App2. You need to identify the minimum number of subnets and
Virtual Network NAT instances required to meet
the following requirements:
• A failure of two zones must NOT affect the availability of either App1 or App2.
• A failure of two zones must NOT affect the outbound connectivity of either App1or App2. What should you identify? To answer, select the appropriate options in
the answer area. NOTE: Each correct selection is worth one point.
A. Mastered
B. Not Mastered
Answer: A

QUESTION 74
- (Exam Topic 3)
Note: This question is part of a series of questions that present the same scenario. Each question in the series contains a unique solution that might meet stated
goals. Some question sets might have more than one correct solution, while others might not have a correct solution.
After you answer a question in this section, you will NOT be able to return to it. As a result, these questions will not appear in the review screen.
You have an Azure subscription that contains the following resources:
* A virtual network named Vnet1
* A subnet named Subnet1 in Vnet1
* A virtual machine named VM1 that connects to Subnet1
* Three storage accounts named storage1, storage2. and storage3
You need to ensure that VM1 can access storage1. VM1 must be prevented from accessing any other storage accounts.
Solution: You create a network security group (NSG). You configure a service tag for MicrosoftStorage and link the tag to Subnet1.
Does this meet the goal?
A. Yes
B. No
Answer: A

QUESTION 75
- (Exam Topic 3)
Note: This question is part of a series of questions that present the same scenario. Each question in the series contains a unique solution that might meet the

stated goals. Some question sets might have more than one correct solution, while others might not have a correct solution.
After you answer a question in this section, you will NOT be able to return to it. As a result, these questions will not appear in the review screen.
You have an Azure application gateway that has Azure Web Application Firewall (WAF) enabled. You configure the application gateway to direct traffic to the URL
of the application gateway.
You attempt to access the URL and receive an HTTP 403 error. You view the diagnostics log and discover the following error.
You need to ensure that the URL is accessible through the application gateway.
Solution: You create a WAF policy exclusion for request headers that contain 137.135.10.24. Does this meet the goal?
A. Yes
B. No
Answer: B

QUESTION 76
- (Exam Topic 3)
You have an Azure virtual network named Vnet1 that connects to an on-premises network. You have an Azure Storage account named storageaccount1 that
contains blob storage.
You need to configure a private endpoint for the blob storage. The solution must meet the following requirements:
Ensure that all on-premises users can access storageaccount1 through the private endpoint.
Prevent access to storageaccount1 from being interrupted.
Which four actions should you perform in sequence? To answer, move the appropriate actions from the list of actions to the answer area and arrange them in the
correct order.
A. Mastered
B. Not Mastered
Answer: A

QUESTION 77
- (Exam Topic 3)
Note: This question is part of a series of questions that present the same scenario. Each question in the series contains a unique solution that might meet the
stated goals. Some question sets might have more than one correct solution, while others might not have a correct solution.
After you answer a question in this section, you will NOT be able to return to it. As a result, these questions will not appear in the review screen.
You have an Azure subscription that contains the following resources:
* A virtual network named Vnet1
* A subnet named Subnet1 in Vnet1
* A virtual machine named VM1 that connects to Subnet1
* Three storage accounts named storage1, storage2, and storage3

You need to ensure that VM1 can access storage1. VM1 must be prevented from accessing any other storage accounts.
Solution: You create a network security group (NSG) and associate the NSG to Subnet1. Does this meet the goal?
A. Yes
B. No
Answer: A

QUESTION 78
- (Exam Topic 3)
Note: This question is part of a series of questions that present the same scenario. Each question in the series contains a unique solution that might meet the
stated goals. Some question sets might have more than one correct solution, while others might not have a correct solution.
After you answer a question in this section, you will NOT be able to return to it. As a result, these questions will not appear in the review screen.
You have an Azure application gateway that has Azure Web Application Firewall (WAF) enabled. You configure the application gateway to direct traffic to the URL
of the application gateway.
You attempt to access the URL and receive an HTTP 403 error. You view the diagnostics log and discover the following error.
You need to ensure that the URL is accessible through the application gateway. Solution: You configure a custom cookie and an exclusion rule.
Does this meet the goal?
A. Yes
B. No
Answer: A

QUESTION 79
- (Exam Topic 3)
Note: This question is part of a series of questions that present the same scenario. Each question in the series contains a unique solution that might meet the
stated goals. Some question sets might have more than one correct solution, while others might not have a correct solution.
After you answer a question in this section, you will NOT be able to return to it. As a result, these questions will not appear in the review screen.
You have two Azure virtual networks named Vnet1 and Vnet2.
You have a Windows 10 device named Client1 that connects to Vnet1 by using a Point-to-Site (P2S) IKEv2 VPN.
You implement virtual network peering between Vnet1 and Vnet2. Vnet1 allows gateway transit. Vnet2 can use the remote gateway.
You discover that Client1 cannot communicate with Vnet2. You need to ensure that Client1 can communicate with Vnet2.
Solution: You download and reinstall the VPN client configuration. Does this meet the goal?
A. Yes
B. No

Answer: A

QUESTION 80

- (Exam Topic 3)

You have an Azure firewall shown in the following exhibit.

Use the drop-down menus to select the answer choice that completes each statement based on the information presented in the graphic.

NOTE: Each correct selection is worth one point.

A. Mastered

B. Not Mastered

Answer: A

QUESTION 81

- (Exam Topic 3)

You have five virtual machines that run Windows Server. Each virtual machine hosts a different web app. You plan to use an Azure application gateway to provide access to each web app by using a hostname of www.contoso.corn and a different URL path for each web app, for example: https://www.contoso.com/app1.

You need to control the flow of traffic based on the URL path. What should you configure?

A. rules

B. rewrites

C. HTTP settings

D. listeners

Answer: A

QUESTION 82

- (Exam Topic 2)

You need to configure GW1 to meet the network security requirements for the P2S VPN users. Which Tunnel type should you select in the Point-to-site configuration settings of GW1?

A. IKEv2 and OpenVPN (SSL)

B. IKEv2

C. IKEv2 and SSTP (SSL)

D. OpenVPN (SSL)

E. SSTP (SSL)

Answer: D

QUESTION 83

- (Exam Topic 1)

You need to provide connectivity to storage1. The solution must meet the PaaS networking requirements and the business requirements.

What should you include in the solution?

A. a service endpoint

B. Azure Front Door

C. a private endpoint

D. Azure Traffic Manager
Answer: A

QUESTION 84
- (Exam Topic 1)
You need to connect Vnet2 and Vnet3. The solution must meet the virtual networking requirements and the business requirements.
Which two actions should you include in the solution? Each correct answer presents part of the solution.
NOTE: Each correct selection is worth one point.
A. On the peerings from Vnet2 and Vnet3, select Use remote gateways.
B. On the peering from Vnet1, select Allow forwarded traffic.
C. On the peering from Vnet1, select Use remote gateways.
D. On the peering from Vnet1, select Allow gateway transit.
E. On the peerings from Vnet2 and Vnet3, select Allow gateway transit.
Answer: BD

QUESTION 85
- (Exam Topic 1)
You need to recommend a configuration for the ExpressRoute connection from the Boston datacenter. The solution must meet the hybrid networking requirements
and business requirements.
What should you recommend? To answer, select the appropriate options in the answer area. NOTE: Each correct selection is worth one point.
A. Mastered
B. Not Mastered
Answer: A

QUESTION 86
- (Exam Topic 3)
You have an Azure subscription that is linked to an Azure Active Directory (Azure AD) tenant named contoso.onmicrosoft.com. The subscription contains the
following resources:
* An Azure App Service app named App1
* An Azure DNS zone named contoso.com
* An Azure private DNS zone named private.contoso.com
* A virtual network named Vnet1
You create a private endpoint for App1. The record for the endpoint is registered automatically in Azure DNS. You need to provide a developer with the name that
is registered in Azure DNS for the private endpoint.
What should you provide?
A. app1.privatelink.azurewebsites.net
B. app1.contoso.com
C. app1.contoso.onmicrosoft.com
D. app1.private.contoso.com
Answer: A

QUESTION 86

- (Exam Topic 3)

You have two Azure virtual networks named Vnet1 and Vnet2 in an Azure region that has three availability zones.

You deploy 12 virtual machines to each virtual network, deploying four virtual machines per zone. The virtual machines in Vnet1 host an app named App1. The virtual machines in Vnet2 host an app named App2.

You plan to use Azure Virtual Network NAT to implement outbound connectivity for App1 and App2. You need to identify the minimum number of subnets and Virtual Network NAT instances required to meet the following requirements:

• A failure of two zones must NOT affect the availability of either App1 or App2.

• A failure of two zones must NOT affect the outbound connectivity of either App1 or App2. What should you identify?

A. Mastered

B. Not Mastered

Answer: A

QUESTION 87

- (Exam Topic 3)

You are planning the IP addressing for the subnets in Azure virtual networks. Which type of resource requires IP addresses in the subnets?

A. internal load balancers

B. storage account

C. serviice endpoints

D. service endpoint policies

Answer: A

QUESTION 88

- (Exam Topic 3)

Note: This question is part of a series of questions that present the same scenario. Each question in the series contains a unique solution that might meet the stated goals. Some question sets might have more than one correct solution, while others might not have a correct solution.

After you answer a question in this section, you will NOT be able to return to it. As a result, these questions will not appear in the review screen.

You have an Azure subscription that contains the following resources:

* A virtual network named Vnet1

* A subnet named Subnet1 in Vnet1

* A virtual machine named VM1 that connects to Subnet1

* Three storage accounts named storage1, storage2, and storage3

You need to ensure that VM1 can access storage1. VM1 must be prevented from accessing any other storage accounts.

Solution: You create a network security group (NSG) and associate the NSG to Subnet1. Does this meet the goal?

A. Yes
B. No
Answer: B

QUESTION 89
- (Exam Topic 3)
Your company has offices in Montreal. Seattle, and Paris. The outbound traffic from each office originates from a specific public IP address.
You create an Azure Front Door instance named FD1 that has Azure Web Application Firewall (WAF) enabled. You configure a WAF policy named Policy! that has
a rule named Rule1. Rule1 applies a rate limit of 100 requests for traffic that originates from the office in Montreal.
You need to apply a rate limit of 100 requests for traffic that originates from each office. What should you do?
A. Modify the conditions of Rule1.
B. Create two additional associations.
C. Modify the rule type of Rule1.
D. Modify the rate limit threshold of Rule1.
Answer: A

QUESTION 90
- (Exam Topic 3)
You have an Azure subscription that contains the public IP addresses shown in the following table.
You plan to deploy a NAT gateway named NAT1.
Which public IP addresses can be used as the public IP address for NAT1?
A. IP3 and IP5 only
B. IP5 only
C. IP1, IP3, and IP5 only
D. IP3 only
E. IP2 and IP4 only
Answer: D

QUESTION 91
You have an Azure application gateway named AppGW1 that balances requests to a web app named App1. You need to modify the server variables in the
response header of App1.
What should you configure on AppGW1?
A. HTTP settings
B. rewrites
C. rules
D. listeners
Answer: B

QUESTION 92
- (Exam Topic 3)

You need to use Traffic Analytics to monitor the usage of applications deployed to Azure virtual machines. Which Azure Network Watcher feature should you implement first?
A. Connection monitor
B. Packet capture
C. NSG flow logs
D. IP flow verify
Answer: A

QUESTION 93
- (Exam Topic 3)
You have the Azure environment shown in the exhibit.
You have virtual network peering between Vnet1 and Vnet2. You have virtual network peering between Vnet4 and Vnet5. The virtual network peering is configured as shown in the following table.
A. Mastered
B. Not Mastered
Answer: A

QUESTION 94
- (Exam Topic 3)
You are planning an Azure Point-to-Site (P2S) VPN that will use OpenVPN. Users will authenticate by using an on premises Active Directory domain. Which additional service should you deploy to support the VPN authentication?
A. a certification authority (CA)
B. a RADIUS server
C. an Azure key vault
D. Azure Active Directory (Azure AD) Application Proxy
Answer: B

QUESTION 95
- (Exam Topic 3)
You have a website that uses an FQDN of www.contoso.com. The DNS record tor www.contoso.com resolves to an on-premises web server.
You plan to migrate the website to an Azure web app named Web1. The website on Web1 will be published by using an Azure Front Door instance named ContosoFD1.
You build the website on Web1.
You plan to configure ContosoFD1 to publish the website for testing.
When you attempt to configure a custom domain for www.contoso.com on ContosoFD1, you receive the error message shown in the exhibit.
You need to test the website and ContosoFD1 without affecting user access to the on-premises web server. Which record should you create in the contoso.com DNS domain?
A. a CNAME record that maps www.contoso.com to ContosoFD1.azurefd.net
B. a CNAME record that maps www.contoso.com to Web1.contoso.com

C. a CNAME record that maps afdverify.www.contoso.com to ContosoFD1.azurefd.net
D. a CNAME record that maps afdverify.www.contoso.com to afdverify.ContosoFD1.azurefd.net
Answer: D

QUESTION 96
- (Exam Topic 3)
You have an Azure Front Door instance that has a single frontend named Frontend1 and an Azure Web Application Firewall (WAF) policy named Policy1. Policy1
redirects requests that have a header containing "string1" to https://www.contoso.com/redirect1. Policy1 is associated to Frontend1.
You need to configure additional redirection settings. Requests to Frontend1 that have a header containing "string2" must be redirected to
https://www.contoso.com/redirect2.
Which three actions should you perform? Each correct answer presents part of the solution. NOTE: Each correct selection is worth one point.
A. Create a custom rule.
B. Configure a managed rule.
C. Create a frontend host.
D. Create a policy.
E. Create an association.
F. Add a custom rule to Policy1.
Answer: ABE

QUESTION 97
- (Exam Topic 3)
You have an Azure virtual network named Vnet1 that has one subnet. Vnet1 is in the West Europe Azure region.
You deploy an Azure App Service app named App1 to the West Europe region.
You need to provide App1 with access to the resources in Vnet1. The solution must minimize costs. What should you do first?
A. Create a private link.
B. Create a new subnet.
C. Create a NAT gateway.
D. Create a gateway subnet and deploy a virtual network gateway.
Answer: B

QUESTION 98
- (Exam Topic 1)
You need to connect Vnet2 and Vnet3. The solution must meet the virtual networking requirements and the business requirements.
Which two actions should you include in the solution? Each correct answer presents part of the solution.
A. On the peerings from Vnet2 and Vnet3, select Use remote gateways.
B. On the peering from Vnet1, select Allow forwarded traffic.
C. On the peering from Vnet1, select Use remote gateways.
D. On the peering from Vnet1, select Allow gateway transit.

E. On the peerings from Vnet2 and Vnet3, select Allow gateway transit.
Answer: BD

QUESTION 99
- (Exam Topic 3)
You have 10 Azure App Service instances. Each instance hosts the same web app. Each instance is in a different Azure region.
You need to configure Azure Traffic Manager to direct users to the instance that has the lowest latency. Which routing method should you use?
A. geographic
B. weighted
C. performance
D. priority
Answer: D

QUESTION 100
- (Exam Topic 3)
Note: This question is part of a series of questions that present the same scenario. Each question in the series contains a unique solution that might meet the
stated goals. Some question sets might have more than one correct solution, while others might not have a correct solution.
After you answer a question in this section, you will NOT be able to return to it. As a result, these questions will not appear in the review screen.
You have two Azure virtual networks named Vnet1 and Vnet2.
You have a Windows 10 device named Client1 that connects to Vnet1 by using a Point-to-Site (P2S) IKEv2 VPN.
You implement virtual network peering between Vnet1 and Vnet2. Vnet1 allows gateway transit. Vnet2 can use the remote gateway.
You discover that Client1 cannot communicate with Vnet2. You need to ensure that Client1 can communicate with Vnet2. Solution: You reset the gateway of
Vnet1.
Does this meet the goal?
A. Yes
B. No
Answer: B

QUESTION 101
- (Exam Topic 3)
You have an Azure virtual network named Vnet1 that has one subnet. Vnet1 is in the West Europe Azure region.
You deploy an Azure App Service app named App1 to the West Europe region.
You need to provide App1 with access to the resources in Vnet1. The solution must minimize costs. What should you do first?
A. Create a private link.
B. Create a new subnet.
C. Create a NAT gateway.

D. Create a gateway subnet and deploy a virtual network gateway.
Answer: B

QUESTION 102
- (Exam Topic 3)
You plan to deploy an Azure virtual network. You need to design the subnets.
Which three types of resources require a dedicated subnet? Each correct answer presents a complete solution. NOTE: Each correct selection is worth one point.
A. VPN gateway
B. Azure Bastion
C. Azure Active Directory Domain Services (Azure AD DS)
D. Azure Application Gateway v2
E. Azure Private Link
Answer: ABD

Chapter 2: Practice Questions & Answers Part 2

QUESTION 103
- (Exam Topic 3)
You have Azure App Service apps in the West US Azure region as shown in the following table.
You need to ensure that all the apps can access the resources in a virtual network named Vnet1 without forwarding traffic through the internet-How many integration subnets should you create?
A. 1
B. 3
C. 4
D. 6
Answer: D

QUESTION 103
- (Exam Topic 3)
You have an Azure virtual network and an on-premises datacenter.
You need to implement a Site-to-Site VPN connection between the datacenter and the virtual network. Which two resources should you create?
A. a virtual network gateway
B. Azure Firewall
C. a local network gateway
D. Azure Web Application Firewall (WAF)
E. an on-premises data gateway
F. an Azure application gateway
G. a user-defined route
Answer: CG

QUESTION 104
- (Exam Topic 3)

You are planning an Azure Point-to-Site (P2S) VPN that will use OpenVPN. Users will authenticate by using an on premises Active Directory domain. Which additional service should you deploy to support the VPN authentication?
A. a certification authority (CA)
B. a RADIUS server
C. an Azure key vault
D. Azure Active Directory (Azure AD) Application Proxy
Answer: B

QUESTION 105
- (Exam Topic 3)
You have an Azure subscription that contains the virtual networks shown in the following table.
You plan to deploy an Azure firewall named AF1 to RG1 in the West US Azure region. To which virtual networks can you deploy AF1?
A. Vnet1 only
B. Vnet1 and Vnet2 only
C. Vnet1, Vnet2, and Vnet4 only
D. Vnet1 and Vnet4 only
E. Vnet1, Vnet2. Vnet3, and Vnet4
Answer: C

QUESTION 106
- (Exam Topic 3)
You have an Azure virtual network named Vnet1.
You need to ensure that the virtual machines in Vnet1 can access only the Azure SQL resources in the East US Azure region. The virtual machines must be prevented from accessing any Azure Storage resources.
Which two outbound network security group (NSG) rules should you create? Each correct answer presents part of the solution.
NOTE: Each correct selection is worth one point.
A. an allow rule that has the IP address range of Vnet1 as the source and destination of Sql.EastUS
B. a deny rule that has a source of VirtualNetwork and a destination of Sql
C. a deny rule that has a source of VirtualNetwork and a destination of 168.63.129.0/24
D. a deny rule that has the IP address range of Vnet1 as the source and destination of Storage
Answer: CD

QUESTION 107
- (Exam Topic 3)
You have an Azure Front Door instance that has a single frontend named Frontend1 and an Azure Web Application Firewall (WAF) policy named Policy1. Policy1 redirects requests that have a header containing "string1" to https://www.contoso.com/redirect1. Policy1 is associated to Frontend1.
You need to configure additional redirection settings. Requests to Frontend1 that have a header containing "string2" must be redirected to https://www.contoso.com/redirect2.

Which three actions should you perform? Each correct answer presents part of the solution. NOTE: Each correct selection is worth one point.
A. Create a custom rule.
B. Configure a managed rule.
C. Create a frontend host.
D. Create a policy.
E. Create an association.
F. Add a custom rule to Policy1.
Answer: ABE

QUESTION 108
- (Exam Topic 3)
Note: This question is part of a series of questions that present the same scenario. Each question in the series contains a unique solution that might meet the
stated goals. Some question sets might have more than one correct solution, while others might not have a correct solution.
After you answer a question in this section, you will NOT be able to return to it. As a result, these questions will not appear in the review screen.
You have an Azure application gateway that has Azure Web Application Firewall (WAF) enabled. You configure the application gateway to direct traffic to the URL
of the application gateway.
You attempt to access the URL and receive an HTTP 403 error. You view the diagnostics log and discover the following error.
You need to ensure that the URL is accessible through the application gateway.
Solution: You create a WAF policy exclusion for request headers that contain 137.135.10.24. Does this meet the goal?
A. Yes
B. No
Answer: B
QUESTION 109
- (Exam Topic 3)
Note: This question is part of a series of questions that present the same scenario. Each question in the series contains a unique solution that might meet the
stated goals. Some question sets might have more than one correct solution, while others might not have a correct solution.
After you answer a question in this section, you will NOT be able to return to it. As a result, these questions will not appear in the review screen.
You have two Azure virtual networks named Vnet1 and Vnet2.
You have a Windows 10 device named Client1 that connects to Vnet1 by using a Point-to-Site (P2S) IKEv2 VPN.
You implement virtual network peering between Vnet1 and Vnet2. Vnet1 allows gateway transit. Vnet2 can use the remote gateway.
You discover that Client1 cannot communicate with Vnet2. You need to ensure that Client1 can communicate with Vnet2. Solution: You enable BGP on the
gateway of Vnet1.
Does this meet the goal?

A. Yes
B. No
Answer: B

QUESTION 110
- (Exam Topic 3)
You are configuring two network virtual appliances (NVAs) in an Azure virtual network. The NVAs will be used to inspect all the traffic within the virtual network.
You need to provide high availability for the NVAs. The solution must minimize administrative effort. What should you include in the solution?
A. Azure Standard Load Balancer
B. Azure Traffic Manager
C. Azure Application Gateway
D. Azure Front Door
Answer: A

QUESTION 111
- (Exam Topic 3)
You have an Azure virtual network named Vnet1 and an on-premises network.
The on-premises network has policy-based VPN devices. In Vnet1, you deploy a virtual network gateway named GW1 that uses a SKU of VpnGw1 and is routebased.
You have a Site-to-Site VPN connection for GW1 as shown in the following exhibit.
You need to ensure that the on-premises network can connect to the route-based GW1. What should you do before you create the connection?
A. Set Use Azure Private IP Address to Enabled
B. Set IPsec / IKE policy to Custom.
C. Set Connection Mode to ResponderOnly
D. Set BGP to Enabled
Answer: A

QUESTION 112
- (Exam Topic 3)
You have an application named App1 that listens for incoming requests on a preconfigured group of 50 TCP ports and UDP ports.
You install App1 on 10 Azure virtual machines.
You need to implement load balancing for App1 across all the virtual machines. The solution must minimize the number of load balancing rules.
What should you include in the solution?
A. Azure Standard Load Balancer that has Floating IP enabled
B. Azure Application Gateway V2 that has multiple listeners
C. Azure Application Gateway v2 that has multiple site hosting enabled
D. Azure Standard Load Balancer that has high availability (HA) ports enabled
Answer: A

QUESTION 113
- (Exam Topic 3)

Note: This question is part of a series of questions that present the same scenario. Each question in the series contains a unique solution that might meet the stated goals. Some question sets might have more than one correct solution, while others might not have a correct solution.

After you answer a question in this section, you will NOT be able to return to it. As a result, these questions will not appear in the review screen.

You have an Azure application gateway that has Azure Web Application Firewall (WAF) enabled. You configure the application gateway to direct traffic to the URL of the application gateway.

You attempt to access the URL and receive an HTTP 403 error. You view the diagnostics log and discover the following error.

You need to ensure that the URL is accessible through the application gateway. Solution: You disable the WAF rule that has a ruleld of 920300.

Does this meet the goal?

A. Yes

B. No

Answer: A

QUESTION 114

- (Exam Topic 3)

You have an Azure subscription that contains an Azure App Service app. The app uses a URL of https://www.contoso.com.

You need to use a custom domain on Azure Front Door for www.contoso.com. The custom domain must use a certificate from an allowed certification authority (CA).

What should you include in the solution?

A. an enterprise application in Azure Active Directory (Azure AD)

B. Active Directory Certificate Services (AD CS)

C. Azure Key Vault

D. Azure Application Gateway

Answer: C

QUESTION 115

- (Exam Topic 3)

You have five virtual machines that run Windows Server. Each virtual machine hosts a different web app. You plan to use an Azure application gateway to provide access to each web app by using a hostname of www.contoso.corn and a different URL path for each web app, for example: https://www.contoso.com/app1.

You need to control the flow of traffic based on the URL path. What should you configure?

A. rules

B. rewrites

C. HTTP settings

D. listeners

Answer: A

QUESTION 116
- (Exam Topic 2)
In which NSGs can you use ASG1 and to which virtual machine network interfaces can you associate ASG1? To answer, select the appropriate options in the
answer area.
NOTE: Each correct selection is worth one point.
A. Mastered
B. Not Mastered
Answer: A

QUESTION 117
- (Exam Topic 2)
You need to meet the network security requirements for the NSG flow logs.
Which type of resource do you need, and how many instances should you create? To answer, select the appropriate options in the answer area.
NOTE: Each correct selection is worth one point.
A. Mastered
B. Not Mastered
Answer: A

QUESTION 118
- (Exam Topic 2)
You are implementing the virtual network requirements for VM Analyze.
What should you include in a custom route that is linked to Subnet2? To answer, select the appropriate options in the answer area.
NOTE: Each correct selection is worth one point.
A. Mastered
B. Not Mastered
Answer: A

QUESTION 119
- (Exam Topic 2)
What should you implement to meet the virtual network requirements for the virtual machines that connect to Vnet4 and Vnet5?
A. a private endpoint
B. a virtual network peering
C. a private link service
D. a routing table
E. a service endpoint
Answer: B

QUESTION 120
- (Exam Topic 3)
You have 10 Azure App Service instances. Each instance hosts the same web app. Each instance is in a different Azure region.

You need to configure Azure Traffic Manager to direct users to the instance that has the lowest latency. Which routing method should you use?
A. geographic
B. weighted
C. performance
D. priority
Answer: D

QUESTION 121
- (Exam Topic 3)
You have an Azure Traffic Manager parent profile named TM1. TM1 has two child profiles named TM2 and TM3.
TM1 uses the performance traffic-routing method and has the endpoints shown in the following table.
TM2 uses the weighted traffic-routing method with MinChildEndpoint = 2 and has the endpoints shown in the following table.
TM3 uses priority traffic-routing method and has the endpoints shown in the following table.
The App2, App4, and App6 endpoints have a degraded monitoring status.
To which endpoint is traffic directed? To answer, select the appropriate options in the answer area.
NOTE: Each correct selection is worth one point
A. Mastered
B. Not Mastered
Answer: A

QUESTION 122
- (Exam Topic 3)
You plan to deploy an Azure virtual network. You need to design the subnets.
Which three types of resources require a dedicated subnet? Each correct answer presents a complete solution. NOTE: Each correct selection is worth one point.
A. VPN gateway
B. Azure Bastion
C. Azure Active Directory Domain Services (Azure AD DS)
D. Azure Application Gateway v2
E. Azure Private Link
Answer: ABD

QUESTION 123
- (Exam Topic 3)
You have the Azure environment shown in the exhibit.
VM1 is a virtual machine that has an instance-level public IP address (ILPIP).
Basic Load Balancer uses a public IP address. VM1 and VM2 are in the backend pool. NAT Gateway uses a public IP address named IP3 that is associated to
SubnetA. VNet1 has a virtual network gateway that has a public IP address named IP4.
When initiating outbound traffic to the internet from VM1, which public address is used?
A. IP1
B. IP2

C. IP3
D. IP4
Answer: A

QUESTION 124
- (Exam Topic 3)
You configure a route table named RT1 that has the routes shown in the following table.
You have an Azure virtual network named Vnet1 that has the subnets shown in the following table.
You have the resources shown in the following table.

Vnet1 connects to an ExpressRoute circuit.
The on-premises router advertises the following routes:
* 0.0.0.0/0
* 10.0.0.0/16
For each of the following statements, select Yes if the statement is true. Otherwise, select No.
NOTE: Each correct selection is worth one point.
A. Mastered
B. Not Mastered
Answer: A

QUESTION 125
- (Exam Topic 3)
You have an Azure application gateway named AppGW1 that provides access to the following hosts:
* www.adatum.com
* www.contoso.com
* www.fabrikam.com
AppGW1 has the listeners shown in the following table.
You create Azure Web Application Firewall (WAF) policies for AppGW1 as shown in the following table.
For each of the following statements, select Yes if the statement is true. Otherwise, select No.
NOTE: Each correct selection is worth one point.

A. Mastered
B. Not Mastered
Answer: A

QUESTION 126
- (Exam Topic 3)
You have an Azure subscription that contains the public IP addresses shown in the following table.
You plan to deploy a NAT gateway named NAT1.
Which public IP addresses can be used as the public IP address for NAT1?
A. IP3 and IP5 only
B. IP5 only
C. IP1, IP3, and IP5 only
D. IP3 only

E. IP2 and IP4 only
Answer: D

QUESTION 127
- (Exam Topic 3)
You have an Azure subscription that contains the resources shown in the following table.
The IP Addresses settings for Vnet1 are configured as shown in the exhibit.

You need to ensure that you can integrate WebApp1 and Vnet1.
Which three actions should you perform in sequence before you can integrate WebApp1 and Vnet1? To answer, move the appropriate actions from the list of actions to the answer area and arrange them in the correct order.
A. Mastered
B. Not Mastered
Answer: A

QUESTION 128
- (Exam Topic 3)
You have an Azure Front Door instance that has a single frontend named Frontend1 and an Azure Web Application Firewall (WAF) policy named Policy1. Policy1 redirects requests that have a header containing "string1" to https://www.contoso.com/redirect1. Policy1 is associated to Frontend1.
You need to configure additional redirection settings. Requests to Frontend1 that have a header containing "string2" must be redirected to https://www.contoso.com/redirect2.
Which three actions should you perform? Each correct answer presents part of the solution. NOTE: Each correct selection is worth one point.
A. Create a custom rule.
B. Configure a managed rule.
C. Create a frontend host.
D. Create a policy.
E. Create an association.
F. Add a custom rule to Policy1.
Answer: ABE

QUESTION 129
- (Exam Topic 3)

You have the Azure Traffic Manager profiles shown in the following table.
You plan to add the endpoints shown in the following table.
Which endpoints can you add to Profile2?
A. Endpoint1 and Endpoint4 only
B. Endpoint1, Endpoint2, Endpoint3, and Endpoint4
C. Endpoint1 only
D. Endpoint2 and Endpoint3 only
E. Endpoint3 only

Answer: A

QUESTION 130

- (Exam Topic 3)

Note: This question is part of a series of questions that present the same scenario. Each question in the series contains a unique solution that might meet stated goals. Some question sets might have more than one correct solution, while others might not have a correct solution.

After you answer a question in this section, you will NOT be able to return to it. As a result, these questions will not appear in the review screen.

You have an Azure subscription that contains the following resources:

* A virtual network named Vnet1
* A subnet named Subnet1 in Vnet1
* A virtual machine named VM1 that connects to Subnet1
* Three storage accounts named storage1, storage2. and storage3

You need to ensure that VM1 can access storage1. VM1 must be prevented from accessing any other storage accounts.

Solution: You create a network security group (NSG). You configure a service tag for MicrosoftStorage and link the tag to Subnet1.

Does this meet the goal?

A. Yes

B. No

Answer: A

QUESTION 131

- (Exam Topic 3)

You have a website that uses an FQDN of www.contoso.com. The DNS record tor www.contoso.com resolves to an on-premises web server.

You plan to migrate the website to an Azure web app named Web1. The website on Web1 will be published by using an Azure Front Door instance named ContosoFD1.

You build the website on Web1.

You plan to configure ContosoFD1 to publish the website for testing.

When you attempt to configure a custom domain for www.contoso.com on ContosoFD1, you receive the error message shown in the exhibit.

You need to test the website and ContosoFD1 without affecting user access to the on-premises web server. Which record should you create in the contoso.com DNS domain?

A. a CNAME record that maps www.contoso.com to ContosoFD1.azurefd.net

B. a CNAME record that maps www.contoso.com to Web1.contoso.com

C. a CNAME record that maps afdverify.www.contoso.com to ContosoFD1.azurefd.net

D. a CNAME record that maps afdverify.www.contoso.com to afdverify.ContosoFD1.azurefd.net

Answer: A

QUESTION 132

- (Exam Topic 3)

You have an Azure subscription that contains the following resources:
A virtual network named Vnet1
Two subnets named subnet1 and AzureFirewallSubnet
A public Azure Firewall named FW1
A route table named RT1 that is associated to Subnet1
A rule routing of 0.0.0.0/0 to FW1 in RT1
After deploying 10 servers that run Windows Server to Subnet1, you discover that none of the virtual machines were activated.
You need to ensure that the virtual machines can be activated. What should you do?
A. On FW1, create an outbound service tag rule for AzureCloud.
B. On FW1, create an outbound network rule that allows traffic to the Azure Key Management Service (KMS).
C. Deploy a NAT gateway.
D. To Subnetl, associate a network security group (NSG) that allows outbound access to port 1688.
Answer: B

QUESTION 133
- (Exam Topic 3)
Note: This question is part of a series of questions that present the same scenario. Each question in the series contains a unique solution that might meet the
stated goals. Some question sets might have more than one correct solution, while others might not have a correct solution.
After you answer a question in this section, you will NOT be able to return to it. As a result, these questions will not appear in the review screen.
You have two Azure virtual networks named Vnet1 and Vnet2.
You have a Windows 10 device named Client1 that connects to Vnet1 by using a Point-to-Site (P2S) IKEv2 VPN.
You implement virtual network peering between Vnet1 and Vnet2. Vnet1 allows gateway transit. Vnet2 can use the remote gateway.
You discover that Client1 cannot communicate with Vnet2. You need to ensure that Client1 can communicate with Vnet2. Solution: You enable BGP on the
gateway of Vnet1.
Does this meet the goal?
A. Yes
B. No
Answer: B

QUESTION 134
- (Exam Topic 3)
You have an Azure virtual network named Vnet1 and an on-premises network.
The on-premises network has policy-based VPN devices. In Vnet1, you deploy a virtual network gateway named GW1 that uses a SKU of VpnGw1 and is routebased.
You have a Site-to-Site VPN connection for GW1 as shown in the following exhibit.
You need to ensure that the on-premises network can connect to the route-based GW1. What should you do before you create the connection?

A. Set Use Azure Private IP Address to Enabled
B. Set IPsec / IKE policy to Custom.
C. Set Connection Mode to ResponderOnly
D. Set BGP to Enabled
Answer: A

QUESTION 135
- (Exam Topic 3)
You have the Azure resources shown in the following table.
You configure storage1 to provide access to the subnet in Vnet1 by using a service endpoint.
You need to ensure that you can use the service endpoint to connect to the read-only endpoint of storage1 in the paired Azure region.
What should you do first?
A. Configure the firewall settings for storage1.
B. Fail over storage1 to the paired Azure region.
C. Create a virtual network in the paired Azure region.
D. Create another service endpoint.
Answer: A

QUESTION 136
- (Exam Topic 3)
Note: This question is part of a series of questions that present the same scenario. Each question in the series contains a unique solution that might meet the
stated goals. Some question sets might have more than one correct solution, while others might not have a correct solution.
After you answer a question in this section, you will NOT be able to return to it. As a result, these questions will not appear in the review screen.
You have an Azure subscription that contains the following resources:
* A virtual network named Vnet1
* A subnet named Subnet1 in Vnet1
* A virtual machine named VM1 that connects to Subnet1
* Three storage accounts named storage1, storage2, and storage3
You need to ensure that VM1 can access storage1. VM1 must be prevented from accessing any other storage accounts.
Solution: You create a network security group (NSG) and associate the NSG to Subnet1. Does this meet the goal?
A. Yes
B. No
Answer: A

QUESTION 137
- (Exam Topic 3)
Note: This question is part of a series of questions that present the same scenario. Each question in the series contains a unique solution that might meet the
stated goals. Some question sets might have more than one correct solution, while others might not have a correct solution.

After you answer a question in this section, you will NOT be able to return to it. As a result, these questions will not appear in the review screen.
You have an Azure application gateway that has Azure Web Application Firewall (WAF) enabled.
You configure the application gateway to direct traffic to the URL
of the application gateway.
You attempt to access the URL and receive an HTTP 403 error. You view the diagnostics log and discover the following error.

You need to ensure that the URL is accessible through the application gateway. Solution: You configure a custom cookie and an exclusion rule.
Does this meet the goal?
A. Yes
B. No
Answer: A

QUESTION 138
- (Exam Topic 3)
Note: This question is part of a series of questions that present the same scenario. Each question in the series contains a unique solution that might meet the
stated goals. Some question sets might have more than one correct solution, while others might not have a correct solution.
After you answer a question in this section, you will NOT be able to return to it. As a result, these questions will not appear in the review screen.
You have two Azure virtual networks named Vnet1 and Vnet2.
You have a Windows 10 device named Client1 that connects to Vnet1 by using a Point-to-Site (P2S) IKEv2 VPN.
You implement virtual network peering between Vnet1 and Vnet2. Vnet1 allows gateway transit. Vnet2 can use the remote gateway.
You discover that Client1 cannot communicate with Vnet2. You need to ensure that Client1 can communicate with Vnet2.
Solution: You download and reinstall the VPN client configuration. Does this meet the goal?
A. Yes
B. No
Answer: A

QUESTION 139
- (Exam Topic 3)
Your company has an on-premises network and three Azure subscriptions named Subscription1, Subscription2, and Subscription3.
The departments at the company use the Azure subscriptions as shown in the following table.
All the resources in the subscriptions are in either the West US Azure region or the West US 2 Azure region. You plan to connect all the subscriptions to the onpremises network by using ExpressRoute.
What is the minimum number of ExpressRoute circuits required?
A. 1
B. 2

C. 3
D. 4
E. 5
Answer: A

QUESTION 140
- (Exam Topic 3)
You need to connect an on-premises network and art Azure environment. The solution must use ExpressRoute and support failing over to a Site-to Site VPN
connection if there is an ExpressRoute failure.
What should you configure? To answer, select the appropriate options in the answer area. NOTE: Each correct selection is worth one point.
A. Mastered
B. Not Mastered
Answer: A

QUESTION 141
- (Exam Topic 3)
You have an Azure subscription that contains two virtual networks named Vnet1 and Vnet2.
You register a public DNS zone named fabrikam.com. The zone is configured as shown in the Public DNS Zone exhibit.
You have a private DNS zone named fabrikam.com. The zone is configured as shown in the Private DNS Zone exhibit.
You have a virtual network link configured as shown in the Virtual Network Link exhibit.
For each of the following statements, select Yes if the statement is true. Otherwise, select No. NOTE: Each correct selection is worth one point.
A. Mastered
B. Not Mastered
Answer: A

QUESTION 142
- (Exam Topic 3)
Note: This question is part of a series of questions that present the same scenario. Each question in the series contains a unique solution that might meet the
stated goals. Some question sets might have more than one correct solution, while others might not have a correct solution.
After you answer a question in this section, you will NOT be able to return to it. As a result, these questions will not appear in the review screen.
You have an Azure application gateway that has Azure Web Application Firewall (WAF) enabled. You configure the application gateway to direct traffic to the URL
of the application gateway.
You attempt to access the URL and receive an HTTP 403 error. You view the diagnostics log and discover the following error.
You need to ensure that the URL is accessible through the application gateway. Solution: You add a rewrite rule for the host header.
Does this meet the goal?

A. Yes
B. No
Answer: B

QUESTION 143
- (Exam Topic 3)
You have an Azure subscription that contains an Azure App Service app. The app uses a URL of https://www.contoso.com.
You need to use a custom domain on Azure Front Door for www.contoso.com. The custom domain must use a certificate from an allowed certification authority
(CA).
What should you include in the solution?
A. an enterprise application in Azure Active Directory (Azure AD)
B. Active Directory Certificate Services (AD CS)
C. Azure Key Vault
D. Azure Application Gateway
Answer: C

QUESTION 144
- (Exam Topic 3)
You have five virtual machines that run Windows Server. Each virtual machine hosts a different web app. You plan to use an Azure application gateway to provide
access to each web app by using a hostname of
www.contoso.corn and a different URL path for each web app, for example: https://www.contoso.com/app1.
You need to control the flow of traffic based on the URL path. What should you configure?
A. rules
B. rewrites
C. HTTP settings
D. listeners
Answer: A

QUESTION 145
- (Exam Topic 3)
You have three on-premises sites. Each site has a third-party VPN device.
You have an Azure virtual WAN named VWAN1 that has a hub named Hub1. Hub1 connects two of the three on-premises sites by using a Site-to-Site VPN
connection.
You need to connect the third site to the other two sites by using Hub1.
Which four actions should you perform in sequence? To answer, move the appropriate actions from the list of actions to the answer area and arrange them in the
correct order.
A. Mastered
B. Not Mastered
Answer: A

QUESTION 146
- (Exam Topic 2)
Which virtual machines can VM1 and VM4 ping successfully? To answer, select the appropriate options in the answer area.
NOTE: Each correct selection is worth one point.
A. Mastered
B. Not Mastered
Answer: A

QUESTION 147
- (Exam Topic 3)
You configure a route table named RT1 that has the routes shown in the following table.
You have an Azure virtual network named Vnet1 that has the subnets shown in the following table.
You have the resources shown in the following table.
Vnet1 connects to an ExpressRoute circuit. The on-premises router advertises the following routes:
* 0.0.0.0/0
* 10.0.0.0/16
For each of the following statements, select Yes if the statement is true. Otherwise, select No.
NOTE: Each correct selection is worth one point.
A. Mastered
B. Not Mastered
Answer: A

QUESTION 148
- (Exam Topic 2)
In which NSGs can you use ASG1 and to which virtual machine network interfaces can you associate ASG1? To answer, select the appropriate options in the
answer area.
NOTE: Each correct selection is worth one point.
A. Mastered
B. Not Mastered
Answer: A

QUESTION 149
- (Exam Topic 1)
You need to implement name resolution for the cloud.liwareinc.com. The solution must meet the networking requirements.
What should you do? To answer, select the appropriate options in the answer area. NOTE: Each correct selection is worth one point.
A. Mastered
B. Not Mastered
Answer: A

QUESTION 150
- (Exam Topic 3)

Note: This question is part of a series of questions that present the same scenario. Each question in the series contains a unique solution that might meet the
stated goals. Some question sets might have more than one correct solution, while others might not have a correct solution.
After you answer a question in this section, you will NOT be able to return to it. As a result, these questions will not appear in the review screen.
You have two Azure virtual networks named Vnet1 and Vnet2.
You have a Windows 10 device named Client1 that connects to Vnet1 by using a Point-to-Site (P2S) IKEv2 VPN.
You implement virtual network peering between Vnet1 and Vnet2. Vnet1 allows gateway transit. Vnet2 can use the remote gateway.
You discover that Client1 cannot communicate with Vnet2. You need to ensure that Client1 can communicate with Vnet2.
Solution: You download and reinstall the VPN client configuration. Does this meet the goal?
A. Yes
B. No
Answer: A

QUESTION 151
- (Exam Topic 3)
Note: This question is part of a series of questions that present the same scenario. Each question in the series contains a unique solution that might meet the
stated goals. Some question sets might have more than one correct solution, while others might not have a correct solution.
After you answer a question in this section, you will NOT be able to return to it. As a result, these questions will not appear in the review screen.
You have an Azure application gateway that has Azure Web Application Firewall (WAF) enabled. You configure the application gateway to direct traffic to the URL
of the application gateway.
You attempt to access the URL and receive an HTTP 403 error. You view the diagnostics log and discover the following error.
You need to ensure that the URL is accessible through the application gateway.
Solution: You create a WAF policy exclusion for request headers that contain 137.135.10.24. Does this meet the goal?
A. Yes
B. No
Answer: B

QUESTION 152
- (Exam Topic 3)
You have an Azure private DNS zone named contoso.com that is linked to the virtual networks shown in the following table.
The links have auto registration enabled.
You create the virtual machines shown in the following table.
You manually add the following entry to the contoso.com zone:
Name: VM1

IP address: 10.1.10.9
For each of the following statements, select Yes of the statement is true. Otherwise, select No. NOTE: Each correct selection is worth one point.

A. Mastered
B. Not Mastered
Answer: A

QUESTION 153
- (Exam Topic 3)
Note: This question is part of a series of questions that present the same scenario. Each question in the series contains a unique solution that might meet stated
goals. Some question sets might have more than one correct solution, while others might not have a correct solution.
After you answer a question in this section, you will NOT be able to return to it. As a result, these questions
will not appear in the review screen.
You have an Azure subscription that contains the following resources:
* A virtual network named Vnet1
* A subnet named Subnet1 in Vnet1
* A virtual machine named VM1 that connects to Subnet1
* Three storage accounts named storage1, storage2. and storage3
You need to ensure that VM1 can access storage1. VM1 must be prevented from accessing any other storage accounts.
Solution: You create a network security group (NSG). You configure a service tag for MicrosoftStorage and link the tag to Subnet1.
Does this meet the goal?
A. Yes
B. No
Answer: B

QUESTION 154
- (Exam Topic 3)
You are planning the IP addressing for the subnets in Azure virtual networks. Which type of resource requires IP addresses in the subnets?
A. Azure Virtual Network NAT
B. virtual network peering
C. service endpoints
D. private endpoints
Answer: A

QUESTION 155
- (Exam Topic 3)
You have an Azure application gateway for a web app named App1. The application gateway allows end-to-end encryption.
You configure the listener for HTTPS by uploading an enterprise signed certificate.

You need to ensure that the application gateway can provide end-to-end encryption for App1. What should you do?
A. Set Listener type to Multi site.
B. Increase the Unhealthy threshold setting in the custom probe.
C. Upload the public key certificate to the HTTPS settings.
D. Enable the SSL profile for the listener.
Answer: C

QUESTION 156
- (Exam Topic 3)
You have an Azure virtual network named Vnet1 and an on-premises network.
The on-premises network has policy-based VPN devices. In Vnet1, you deploy a virtual network gateway named GW1 that uses a SKU of VpnGw1 and is routebased.
You have a Site-to-Site VPN connection for GW1 as shown in the following exhibit.
You need to ensure that the on-premises network can connect to the route-based GW1. What should you do before you create the connection?
A. Set Use Azure Private IP Address to Enabled
B. Set IPsec / IKE policy to Custom.
C. Set Connection Mode to ResponderOnly
D. Set BGP to Enabled
Answer: A

QUESTION 157
- (Exam Topic 3)
You are configuring two network virtual appliances (NVAs) in an Azure virtual network. The NVAs will be used to inspect all the traffic within the virtual network.
You need to provide high availability for the NVAs. The solution must minimize administrative effort. What should you include in the solution?
A. Azure Standard Load Balancer
B. Azure Traffic Manager
C. Azure Application Gateway
D. Azure Front Door
Answer: A

QUESTION 158
- (Exam Topic 3)
You have an Azure virtual network and an on-premises datacenter.
You need to implement a Site-to-Site VPN connection between the datacenter and the virtual network. Which two resources should you create? Each correct answer presents part of the solution. NOTE: Each correct selection is worth one point.
A. a virtual network gateway
B. Azure Firewall
C. a local network gateway
D. Azure Web Application Firewall (WAF)
E. an on-premises data gateway

F. an Azure application gateway
G. a user-defined route
Answer: AC

QUESTION 159
- (Exam Topic 3)
Note: This question is part of a series of questions that present the same scenario. Each question in the series contains a unique solution that might meet the
stated goals. Some question sets might have more than one correct solution, while others might not have a correct solution.
After you answer a question in this section, you will NOT be able to return to it. As a result, these questions will not appear in the review screen.
You have an Azure application gateway that has Azure Web Application Firewall (WAF) enabled. You configure the application gateway to direct traffic to the URL
of the application gateway.
You attempt to access the URL and receive an HTTP 403 error. You view the diagnostics log and discover the following error.
You need to ensure that the URL is accessible through the application gateway. Solution: You configure a custom cookie and an exclusion rule.
Does this meet the goal?
A. Yes
B. No
Answer: A

QUESTION 160
- (Exam Topic 3)
You plan to configure BGP for a Site-to-Site VPN connection between a datacenter and Azure. Which two Azure resources should you configure? Each correct
answer presents a part of the solution.
(Choose two.)
NOTE: Each correct selection is worth one point.
A. a virtual network gateway
B. Azure Application Gateway
C. Azure Firewall
D. a local network gateway
E. Azure Front Door
Answer: AD

QUESTION 161
- (Exam Topic 3)
You have an Azure subscription that contains multiple virtual machines in the West US Azure region. You need to use Traffic Analytics.
Which two resources should you create? Each correct answer presents part of the solution. (Choose two.) NOTE: Each correct answer selection is worth one
point.
A. an Azure Monitor workbook

B. a Log Analytics workspace C a storage account
C. an Azure Sentinel workspace
D. an Azure Monitor data collection rule
Answer: BC

QUESTION 162
- (Exam Topic 3)
You have two Azure virtual networks named Hub1 and Spoke1. Hub1 connects to an on-premises network by using a Site-to-Site VPN connection.
You are implementing peering between Hub1 and Spoke1.
You need to ensure that a virtual machine connected to Spoke1 can connect to the on-premises network through Hub1.
How should you complete the PowerShell script? To answer, drag the appropriate values to the correct targets. Each value may be used once, more than once, or
not at all. You may need to drag the split bar between panes or scroll to view content.
NOTE: Each correct selection is worth one point.
A. Mastered
B. Not Mastered
Answer: A

QUESTION 163
- (Exam Topic 3)
You have an Azure virtual network that contains two subnets named Subnet1 and Subnet2. Subnet1 contains a virtual machine named VM1. Subnet2 contains a
virtual machine named VM2.
You have two network security groups (NSGs) named NSG1 and NSG2. NSG1 has 100 inbound security rules and is associated to VM1. NSG2 has 200 inbound
security rules and is associated to Subnet1.
VM2 cannot connect to VM1.
You suspect that an NSG rule blocks connectivity.
You need to identify which rule blocks the connection. The issue must be resolved as quickly as possible. Which Azure Network Watcher feature should you use?
A. Effective security rules
B. Connection troubleshoot
C. NSG diagnostic
D. NSG flow logs
Answer: C

QUESTION 164
- (Exam Topic 3)
You have an Azure virtual network named Vnet1 that has one subnet. Vnet1 is in the West Europe Azure region.
You deploy an Azure App Service app named App1 to the West Europe region.
You need to provide App1 with access to the resources in Vnet1. The solution must minimize costs. What should you do first?
A. Create a private link.

B. Create a new subnet.
C. Create a NAT gateway.
D. Create a gateway subnet and deploy a virtual network gateway.
Answer: B

QUESTION 165
- (Exam Topic 3)
Note: This question is part of a series of questions that present the same scenario. Each question in the series contains a unique solution that might meet the
stated goals. Some question sets might have more than one correct solution, while others might not have a correct solution.
After you answer a question in this section, you will NOT be able to return to it. As a result, these questions will not appear in the review screen.
You have an Azure application gateway that has Azure Web Application Firewall (WAF) enabled.
You configure the application gateway to direct traffic to the URL of the application gateway.
You attempt to access the URL and receive an HTTP 403 error. You view the diagnostics log and discover the following error.
You need to ensure that the URL is accessible through the application gateway.
Solution: You create a WAF policy exclusion request headers that contain 137.135.10.24. Does this meet the goat?
A. Yes
B. No
Answer: B

QUESTION 166
- (Exam Topic 1)
You need to connect Vnet2 and Vnet3. The solution must meet the virtual networking requirements and the business requirements.
Which two actions should you include in the solution? Each correct answer presents part of the solution.
A. On the peerings from Vnet2 and Vnet3, select Use remote gateways.
B. On the peering from Vnet1, select Allow forwarded traffic.
C. On the peering from Vnet1, select Use remote gateways.
D. On the peering from Vnet1, select Allow gateway transit.
E. On the peerings from Vnet2 and Vnet3, select Allow gateway transit.
Answer: BD

QUESTION 167
- (Exam Topic 3)
You have 10 Azure App Service instances. Each instance hosts the same web app. Each instance is in a different Azure region.
You need to configure Azure Traffic Manager to direct users to the instance that has the lowest latency. Which routing method should you use?
A. geographic
B. weighted
C. performance

D. priority
Answer: D

QUESTION 168
- (Exam Topic 3)
Note: This question is part of a series of questions that present the same scenario. Each question in the series contains a unique solution that might meet the
stated goals. Some question sets might have more than one correct solution, while others might not have a correct solution.
After you answer a question in this section, you will NOT be able to return to it. As a result, these questions will not appear in the review screen.
You have two Azure virtual networks named Vnet1 and Vnet2.
You have a Windows 10 device named Client1 that connects to Vnet1 by using a Point-to-Site (P2S) IKEv2 VPN.
You implement virtual network peering between Vnet1 and Vnet2. Vnet1 allows gateway transit. Vnet2 can use the remote gateway.
You discover that Client1 cannot communicate with Vnet2. You need to ensure that Client1 can communicate with Vnet2. Solution: You reset the gateway of
Vnet1.
Does this meet the goal?
A. Yes
B. No
Answer: B

QUESTION 169
- (Exam Topic 3)
You have an Azure virtual network named Vnet1 that has one subnet. Vnet1 is in the West Europe Azure region.
You deploy an Azure App Service app named App1 to the West Europe region.
You need to provide App1 with access to the resources in Vnet1. The solution must minimize costs. What should you do first?
A. Create a private link.
B. Create a new subnet.
C. Create a NAT gateway.
D. Create a gateway subnet and deploy a virtual network gateway.
Answer: B

QUESTION 170
- (Exam Topic 3)
You have an Azure Traffic Manager parent profile named TM1. TM1 has two child profiles named TM2 and TM3.
TM1 uses the performance traffic-routing method and has the endpoints shown in the following table.
TM2 uses the weighted traffic-routing method with MinChildEndpoint = 2 and has the endpoints shown in the following table.
TM3 uses priority traffic-routing method and has the endpoints shown in the following table.

The App2, App4, and App6 endpoints have a degraded monitoring status.
To which endpoint is traffic directed? To answer, select the appropriate options in the answer area.
NOTE: Each correct selection is worth one point
A. Mastered
B. Not Mastered
Answer: A

QUESTION 171
- (Exam Topic 3)
You plan to deploy an Azure virtual network. You need to design the subnets.
Which three types of resources require a dedicated subnet? Each correct answer presents a complete solution. NOTE: Each correct selection is worth one point.
A. VPN gateway
B. Azure Bastion
C. Azure Active Directory Domain Services (Azure AD DS)
D. Azure Application Gateway v2
E. Azure Private Link
Answer: ABD

QUESTION 172
- (Exam Topic 3)
You have Azure App Service apps in the West US Azure region as shown in the following table.
You need to ensure that all the apps can access the resources in a virtual network named Vnet1 without forwarding traffic through the internet-How many
integration subnets should you create?
A. 1
B. 3
C. 4
D. 6
Answer: D

QUESTION 173
- (Exam Topic 3)
You have an Azure virtual network and an on-premises datacenter.
You need to implement a Site-to-Site VPN connection between the datacenter and the virtual network. Which two resources should you create? Each correct
answer presents part of the solution. NOTE: Each
correct selection is worth one point.
A. a virtual network gateway
B. Azure Firewall
C. a local network gateway
D. Azure Web Application Firewall (WAF)
E. an on-premises data gateway
F. an Azure application gateway
G. a user-defined route
Answer: CG

QUESTION 174

- (Exam Topic 3)

You are planning an Azure Point-to-Site (P2S) VPN that will use OpenVPN. Users will authenticate by using an on premises Active Directory domain. Which additional service should you deploy to support the VPN authentication?

A. a certification authority (CA)
B. a RADIUS server
C. an Azure key vault
D. Azure Active Directory (Azure AD) Application Proxy

Answer: B

QUESTION 175

- (Exam Topic 3)

You have an Azure subscription that contains the virtual networks shown in the following table. You plan to deploy an Azure firewall named AF1 to RG1 in the West US Azure region. To which virtual networks can you deploy AF1?

A. Vnet1 only
B. Vnet1 and Vnet2 only
C. Vnet1, Vnet2, and Vnet4 only
D. Vnet1 and Vnet4 only
E. Vnet1, Vnet2. Vnet3, and Vnet4

Answer: C

QUESTION 176

- (Exam Topic 3)

You have an Azure subscription.
You have the on-premises sites shown the following table.
You plan to deploy Azure Virtual WAN.
You are evaluating Virtual WAN Basic and Virtual WAN Standard.
Which type of Virtual WAN can you use for each site? To answer, select the appropriate options in the answer area.
NOTE: Each correct selection is worth one point.

A. Mastered
B. Not Mastered

Answer: A

ONLINE RESOURCES

Practice Paper
Link : https://forms.gle/fuKFwsTqXFGAcz718

QR Code :

Video Content

Link :
https://www.youtube.com/playlist?list=PLzlh_31VWEFowujgDl16YDCvsQtmKgEqL

QR Code :

Chapter 3: Viva Voce Questions

Q 1: What is Microsoft Azure Networking?
Answer: Microsoft Azure Networking is a collection of cloud-based networking services and solutions designed to provide secure and scalable network infrastructure for applications running in Azure.
Q 2: What is a Virtual Network (VNet) in Azure?
Answer: A Virtual Network (VNet) in Azure provides a private network in the cloud where you can provision your services and VMs securely.
Q 3: Can you explain subnetting in Azure VNets?
Answer: Subnetting in Azure VNets involves dividing a VNet into multiple sub-networks, allowing for organized allocation of IP addresses and security segmentation.
Q 4: What are Network Security Groups (NSGs) in Azure?
Answer: NSGs are used to filter network traffic to and from Azure resources in a VNet. They can contain multiple inbound and outbound security rules that allow or deny traffic based on several parameters.
Q 5: Describe Azure Load Balancer.
Answer: Azure Load Balancer is a Layer-4 (TCP, UDP) traffic management solution that provides high availability and network performance to your applications.
Q 6: What is Azure Application Gateway?
Answer: Azure Application Gateway is a web traffic load balancer that enables you to manage traffic to your web applications. It includes features like SSL termination, cookie-based session affinity, and URL-based routing.
Q 7: How does Azure VPN Gateway function?
Answer: Azure VPN Gateway connects your on-premises networks to Azure through Site-to-Site VPNs, enabling secure and reliable connectivity over the internet.
Q 8: Explain the purpose of Azure ExpressRoute.
Answer: Azure ExpressRoute allows for a private connection between Azure data centers and infrastructure on-premises or in a colocation environment, bypassing the internet for enhanced security and reliability.
Q 9: What is Azure Front Door?
Answer: Azure Front Door is a scalable and secure entry point for web applications, providing global load balancing and site acceleration.
Q 10: Discuss the Azure Traffic Manager.
Answer: Azure Traffic Manager is a DNS-based traffic load balancer that distributes traffic optimally to services across global Azure regions to provide high availability and responsiveness.
Q 11: What is Network Peering in Azure?
Answer: Network peering involves connecting two Azure VNets, enabling resources in one VNet to communicate directly with resources in another VNet.
Q 12: Can you describe Azure Bastion?

Answer: Azure Bastion provides secure and seamless RDP/SSH connectivity to your virtual machines directly from the Azure portal over SSL.

Q 13: How do you implement DDoS protection in Azure?

Answer: Azure provides DDoS Protection Standard, which enhances security by mitigating DDoS attacks and protecting resources in Azure Virtual Networks.

Q 14: What are Azure Private Links?

Answer: Azure Private Link allows you to access Azure services securely over a private endpoint in your VNet, minimizing exposure to the public internet.

Q 15: Explain the use of Azure Route Tables.

Answer: Azure Route Tables, or user-defined routes (UDR), are used to define how traffic is routed in a VNet, providing control over traffic flow within subnets.

Q 16: What is Azure Firewall?

Answer: Azure Firewall is a managed, cloud-based network security service that protects your Azure Virtual Network resources. It is a stateful firewall as a service with built-in high availability.

Q 17: How does Azure monitor and manage network performance?

Answer: Azure provides multiple tools like Azure Monitor and Network Watcher that help monitor and diagnose conditions at a network scenario level.

Q 18: What are service endpoints in Azure?

Answer: Service endpoints extend your VNet private address space and the identity of your VNet to Azure services, securing and isolating access to Azure service resources.

Q 19: How is network connectivity managed between Azure and other cloud services?

Answer: Connectivity can be managed using various services like Azure ExpressRoute, VPN Gateways, or through peering arrangements to ensure secure and reliable interconnectivity.

Q 20: What role does Azure DNS play in networking?

Answer: Azure DNS is a hosting service for DNS domains, providing name resolution using Microsoft Azure infrastructure.

YouTube Link for Viva Voce Questions:
https://www.youtube.com/playlist?list=PLzlh_31VWEFpGJhWiuJoAgMxbfW4sX8Mc

QR Code:

YouTube Videos Playlists for all Microsoft Certifications Videos

Microsoft Azure AI Fundamentals AZ-900
Link: https://www.youtube.com/playlist?list=PLzlh_31VWEFq9KU8Gr0ISbfj-TW6k17f8

QR Code:

Microsoft Azure Administrator AZ-104   Microsoft Azure Virtual Desktop AZ-140
Link: https://www.youtube.com/playlist?list=PLzlh_31VWEFq7JHJMuPJZcw-XShaPrUYP

QR Code:

Microsoft Azure Virtual Desktop AZ-140
Link: https://www.youtube.com/playlist?list=PLzlh_31VWEFowmPK_ro41wiljGoGKexGI

QR Code:

Microsoft Azure Developer AZ-204
Link:
https://www.youtube.com/playlist?list=PLzlh_31VWEFqT72UPVCUi6rqRqLBuwMSr

QR Code:

Designing Microsoft Azure Infrastructure Solution AZ-305
Link:
https://www.youtube.com/playlist?list=PLzlh_31VWEFpTerOknh9kgL4eTbhQwDND

QR Code:

Microsoft Azure Devops Engineer AZ-400
Link: https://www.youtube.com/playlist?list=PLzlh_31VWEFpyUIe_DuaeIkcThEfMT_BT

QR Code:

Microsoft Azure Security Engineer AZ-500
Link:
https://www.youtube.com/playlist?list=PLzlh_31VWEFqFBJgQTPNucIO0wVJdjNmS

QR Code:

Microsoft Azure Network Engineer AZ-700
Link:
https://www.youtube.com/playlist?list=PLzlh_31VWEFowujgDl16YDCvsQtmKgEqL

QR Code:

Microsoft Azure Fundamentals AZ-900
Link: https://www.youtube.com/playlist?list=PLzlh_31VWEFpeXZ2p32R1zDsgcbV8kI1K

QR Code:

Microsoft Azure Data Engineer DP-203
Link: https://www.youtube.com/playlist?list=PLzlh_31VWEFp3XTNqoS60UAOzl8NVG-5z

QR Code:

Microsoft Azure Database Administrator DP- 300
Link: https://www.youtube.com/playlist?list=PLzlh_31VWEFpv-rmc2mbpoIqUOqVW_cIo

QR Code: